AMY

# Easyish:

## KEYS TO A (RELATIVELY) EASY RELATIONSHIP

ISBN: 978-1-7357805-0-4 (paperback)
ISBN: 978-1-7357805-1-1 (e-book)

Printed in USA

Cover and book design by Asya Blue Design

www.easyishbook.com

This book is dedicated, with so much love and sincere appreciation, to my husband, Rodney. Thank you for your steadfast belief in me, in us, and in this project. You have been after me to write this since the day we met. Thank you for showing me that the relationship I had imagined was possible actually is. Thank you for allowing me to be free. Thank you for your kindness and patience, and for the seemingly endless supply of radical grace you offer. Thank you for doing this family life with me. You're my favorite person I ever met. "Ain't no divorce!"
#MPG5L

Thank you also to my trusted advisors, Jennifer Drake and Emiel Barrett, for your support and encouragement. You've challenged and supported me with humor and patience every step of the way. Thank you thank you thank you! I love you guys.

Thank you to my parents, who were two of my earliest readers, and who have always encouraged my writing. I am grateful to have been raised by such smart, thoughtful humans who showed me that divorce can be done well.

# INTRO TO
# EASY*ISH:* KEYS TO A
# (RELATIVELY) EASY
# RELATIONSHIP

*I am a Relationship Counselor.*

I've always been fascinated by relationships. I'm always thinking about people and how we relate to one another. I want to know how and why we connect, as well as how and why we disconnect. I'm always curious about what makes people fall in love, and then once they're in, what makes them fall out of love. Trying to figure out *what this person might be thinking or feeling that's making them act this way* is my favorite mental game. I'm fascinated by relationships. All of them. I'm just as interested in the functional as the dysfunctional. *What makes this one work, but this one doesn't? Why is this relationship so hard, where this one is pretty smooth and easy?* I have always wanted to find and understand the keys to relationship success.

So I became a Relationship Counselor.

What this means is that people generally come to me when their relationships are in real trouble. They come to me when they are mired in conflict, when there has been infidelity, when trust is broken. They come to me when they've been married for twenty years and raised their kids and suddenly find they have nothing to talk about. People come to me when they have stopped communicating, when they've stopped having sex, or when they've fought the same fight too many times and they've all but given up.

Now, my website states very clearly that I AM NOT A MAGICIAN. (It literally says that.) Because the truth is: I can't magically heal whatever wounds your relationship has sustained. It is important that my clients have realistic expectations and understand that I can't take away years of stonewalling and contempt, defensiveness and criticism. *(*Leading marriage researcher John Gottman refers to these as the "Four Horsemen of the Apocalypse," because his research has demonstrated that they are harbingers of pending divorce.)* I can't do the work for you.

You see, in order for me to be most effective, it would be better for people to come after the *first* fight. After the *first* failure to apologize. I want clients to reach out for help after the *first* miscommunication, so that they can learn how to effectively communicate and thereby avoid the erosion of continual misunderstanding. I want people to get help when *trust is still intact*. I say this because it is relatively easy to repair a crack, especially when it first begins to show, but it is nearly impossible to repair a break. Once you're at a certain point of disintegration, the "work" becomes a thankless uphill trudge that goes nowhere and feels dissatisfying and fruitless.

I want people to consider Relationship Counseling and the intentional building of communication skills to be accessible, normal, healthy, and even necessary for relationship success. Because while relationships can be challenging, they should ultimately be a source of great joy and happiness. When they are not, there is work to be done. The thing is, though, any work you put in should feel *satisfying and worthwhile*.

Another intention in writing this book is to give people hope that a relationship isn't doomed if it's hard, *if what is missing are merely skills*, which can be taught. But it's important to understand that I can give you all the skills in the world, and that won't necessarily make you and another person a good fit. I will continuously stress the idea that goodness-of-fit, when it comes to basic temperament, is a real thing and should be considered.

Yet another goal in writing this is to highlight the need for a solid development of the self first. In order to show up to your relationships with others as your best and highest version, it is crucial that you are intentional and clear in your relationship with your self. You must fully understand who you are and where you come from, as well as what triggers, challenges, and delights you. Many of us have never stopped to deeply consider the questions of, *"Who am I? What is important to me? What do I believe in?"* My hope is that digging in and beginning to better understand these aspects of yourself will help clarify what you want in a long-term relationship, or possibly marriage, with someone else. You have to do the work *there* in order to find ease anywhere.

There are all manner of resources out there to help take your relationship, with yourself and eventually with your person, to the next level. Furthermore, when it comes to the relationships you choose, I also want you to come away with an acceptance that there's no shame in throwing in the proverbial towel when it's clear that the time has come. I will offer you some tools to make your relationships with others easier, and I hope you'll have the curiosity to explore them in whatever ways work for you, and find the strength, courage, and confidence to leave them if that is what's best.

I absolutely know that all parts of this book won't resonate with everyone. How could they? I am only able to write from my own perspective and tell you what I've learned from my life and from my clients' lives. *(So, please offer me some grace if you sense a blind spot, and trust that I'm a work in progress.)* My intention is to honor and celebrate all of your identities, in all your different relationships, and offer something for everyone that can help you build the relationships you want and deserve. I want all of you to have access to any wisdom or guidance that can help you lead your best and fullest life, whatever that looks like for you!

I say all that to say: *please cherry-pick!* These keys won't unlock every door for every reader. Think of this book like I'm handing you a big ol' ring full of different sizes, colors, and shapes of keys, like the one the manager of a large building always seems to have dangling from their belt. You can picture this, yes? It's impossible to know exactly which key is for which door, so there's likely to be a lot of trial and error finding the right one. You can expect it is going to take some time and effort to test each key and see if it unlocks something *for you*.

Kafka wrote, *"Many a book is like a key to unknown chambers within the castle of one's own self."* In other words, I simply encourage you to use this content in whatever way works for you. Take what resonates and leave the rest entirely. *(My ex-girlfriend and I used to go to dinner with her parents a lot, and her dad would always say, "Order what you want, and if you hate it, throw it against the wall!" Obviously, no one ever threw anything against the wall in public, but the advice was on point: if it doesn't taste good, don't eat it!)*

If you stick with me, there will be loads of practical tips and tools, but also "homework" in the form of reflection questions you can do alone or with a partner. Whether you choose to do them is, of course, up to you. My guess is you'll have a better shot at unlocking something if you do, but whatever you choose, please use this book for your own unique purposes. Reject what doesn't resonate or feel authentic to you. That's my first lesson for you, to be broadly applied. You do you, whatever that looks like, and know that you can't really do it wrong.

My ultimate goal is to offer you one possible path to the easy*ish* relationship you want and deserve. I sincerely hope this helps, and I can't wait to hear about it if it does! If it doesn't, well, throw it against the wall.

Welcome to Easy*ish:* Keys To A (Relatively) Easy Relationship

~Amy L. Miller, MSW, LCSW~

# TABLE OF CONTENTS:

**Part One: Relationship With Self**

**Part Two: Relationship With Someone Else**

# PART ONE:

# RELATIONSHIP WITH SELF

# LESSON 1: WHO AM I?

...And then there's me and the question of why I care so much about all of this. Besides the fact that it's literally my job to study and understand relationships, the simplest answer is that I'm the sort of person who can't intellectualize anything. I have to try it on and walk around in it to figure out whether it works for me or not. So I've been spending my entire life trying to figure out relationships, which includes plenty of practice in the wrong ones.

*"I'm not upset that you lied to me, I'm upset that from now on I can't believe you."*
— Friedrich Nietzsche

Fun fact: I dated a **legit, real-life pathological liar** once.

I use bold and italics to emphasize that this man lied about literally everything, for no apparent reason. He was incredibly convincing and truly remarkable in his ability to hold all the stories at once and weave them together and live according to the "facts" of his life, considering they were mostly not remotely true.

That's why I didn't use the famous Mark Twain quote, *"...If you tell the truth you don't have to remember anything..."* He didn't have the problem of not being consistent, or of forgetting what he lied about. He was rather brilliant in this way. My best understanding in retrospect is that he was a very wounded, dysfunctional, sensitive, and creative man who made up really good stories, only instead of just thinking about them or writing novels, he tried to live them like they were true.

Examples: He made up a brother and a best friend to account for his broken relationships. He lied about his age because I told him the last guy I dated was too old. He invented a stolen truck to account for not having transport. He pretended to go to work every day and fabricated a story about the banking errors that kept money from getting successfully into his account.

I'm telling you: the whole thing was convincing and elaborate. I pride myself on having an unimpeachable BS meter and impeccable intuition, but somehow, this man and his incredible ability to fabricate the truth slipped past all my alarm systems. I think he was so good at lying that *he* actually didn't believe he was lying, which made it almost undetectable to me. He was also a brilliant writer, which I'm a sucker for. His way with written words and how they made me feel to read decidedly impacted my willingness to believe him.

I started thinking about this man recently when Facebook memories reminded me of that summer when I was finally starting to piece together the fragments of the truth. I remember it being very painful. He had been living with me for about two months at this point, and so clearly I trusted him not only with my heart but with my space and my belongings. And he not only lied to me, and invaded my privacy, but he also stole from me. Multiple times. I didn't find this out for sure until after he'd already gone, but it was just adding insult to injury at that point.

So, obviously this goes without saying: *that really sucked*. It was not a good, safe, or healthy relationship situation. I had been roundly duped and I felt incredibly stupid. I felt ashamed that I'd fallen for what was so obviously an elaborate con. I had opened my home to this person because he'd led me to believe it was safe to do that. I felt betrayed. It made me doubt myself and my ability to judge character.

But at the same time, I didn't want to tell anybody what had really happened because I didn't want people to judge him harshly. I wanted to protect him. I felt...sorry for him. I felt empathy. I felt pity. I remember thinking, *"My god, how terrible must he be feeling about his actual life to just invent a whole new one?"*

I also felt angry and sad. I was grieving an idea. There was suddenly a huge expanse of space in my life where there hadn't been before, because he'd been in my life every day. I had gotten used to him, so when he was suddenly gone, I missed him. I felt dumb for missing him, because he didn't deserve to be missed, and also what was I even missing? I'd been tricked. He wasn't even real. I remember feeling just completely overwhelmed with all of this.

All the feelings were competing for leverage. It was hard to say, day by day, hour by hour, what the truest feelings were. It took a long time to move past it. I actually gave him another chance at one point, which was also incredibly stupid in retrospect, but I felt like he deserved it at the time. I thought I could "fix" him. *(I couldn't. Newsflash: We can't fix people.)*

Eventually it became unarguably evident that he was a deeply disturbed and damaged person, and that in spite of the beauty I saw in him (and believe was there), it wasn't going to go anywhere. The relationship had no foundation of trust, so it had no future. But nobody could have told me that; believe me, they tried. But as is often the case, I had to learn *for myself* that he was not my problem nor my responsibility, and that is what took a while. It is embarrassing to tell this story, now that I'm older and wiser.

BUT.

You know what? I am glad the whole thing happened. As ridiculous as that may sound given the pain and humiliation, I learned so much from it. I wouldn't trade it in, even if I could. Not even to get back what he stole, or to get back the time I wasted. It was a lesson. It was my life. It was one of the many steps on the path to learning a hard lesson that the universe was going to continue teaching me over and over until I stopped doing the same things. My main lesson here was this:

*HEY AMY! GUESS WHAT?! Stop trying to fix people. Focus on your own problems. Find someone healthy to be with.*

Funnily enough, not very many people know the details of this story. It's been long enough now that the sting is gone, but honestly, I felt really stupid for having been in this situation at all, much less for it taking me so long to fully extricate myself. But I am willing to tell you about this because it is important to me that you all know that I have made quite a few messes in my life. I learn pretty much everything the hard way, and I have tried on every version of relationship out there. So you are in good company if you too have a bit of a, shall we say, *convoluted* history.

Just a heads up that I will share a fair amount about my own life and relationships here, much more than I would share in a counseling session. I will say, however, that unlike many more-traditional therapists, I do self-disclose quite a bit in general. I find sharing with clients to be rapport-building; I've found people like to know that not only am I real, but I struggle with the same things they do. It can be powerful to normalize an experience a client is having by explaining how I navigated something similar. Often, how I make sense of things my clients are dealing with is through reflection on my own life and how I've handled things, or imagining how I might feel in certain situations. The same might be true for you, so my hope is that my stories will help you.

And I have a lot of stories! I was married once before, to a man. Prior to that, I lived with a female partner for several years. Someone I dated when they identified as a lesbian has since come out as transgender, which in retrospect makes a lot of sense for them. I've dated people older and younger than me, of various races and ethnicities. All different personality types and circumstances, including people with children, emotionally unavailable men, and a brief and long-distance affair with a married man. I've had a lot of sex, not all of which was for the right reasons, and not all of which I enjoyed.

I've used all the dating apps that were available at the time. I've been on a lot of first dates.

Some of this experimentation worked pretty well; some of it was disastrous. I've made a lot of bad decisions and some risky mistakes. I've hurt people who sincerely loved me, and I've been deeply hurt. I've tried it all, because I *just have to find out for myself.* I have always wanted to understand people and relationships, and this is the path I've taken to learn. I'm not sure I'd recommend it, but here we are. Through it all, I've been asking myself questions about relationships, and revising my understanding with every new piece of information or experience.

Questions like:

*How do relationships work, in theory?*

*How do relationships work for other people?*

*How/DO relationships work for me?*

*What makes them healthy?*

*Why do some feel so hard?*

*Is it worth staying when they do?*

*Will I ever find a place to land and stay?*

*How do I know when it's time to move on?*

*Am I being unreasonable by expecting my relationship to be easyish most of the time?*

I've also spent my life asking questions about myself. Questions like:

*Who am I?*

*What are my values?*

*What do I believe?*

*What is my purpose?*

*What makes me happy?*

*What do I need?*

*What nourishes my spirit?*

*How do I communicate?*

*What is the best way to authentically express myself?*

*Who "gets" me?*

*What are my boundaries?*

*What do I struggle with?*

I've learned a lot about myself over the years. And I think it's fair to say that my greatest relationship challenge has been trying to figure out how to get what I needed without sacrificing my identity and autonomy. It is hard for me to give of myself; I'm pretty selfish in some ways. It is really hard for me to share space. It is hard for me to ask for help. I am restless and I struggle to stay put. I desperately want roots but I fear anchors. I resent feeling "stuck."

It is challenging for me to be monogamous, particularly when it comes to emotional intimacy. My entire adulthood, I've been trying to determine whether one person could be enough for me, whether I could be enough for them, and whether a long-term relationship, *much less marriage*, is plausible for me.

At this writing, my husband and I have been married for a few years and it is working great, but in order for that to be possible, I've had to reframe the very notion of marriage. We also have to communicate a *lot*. As I mentioned, and I'll say more about this later, I was married once before and it didn't feel right. We only lasted one year. For a long time post-divorce, I was decidedly against the idea of doing it again.

To make it work for us now, we have had to negotiate. We have had to very intentionally and collaboratively transform marriage into what works for us, rather than conform to what society tells us it *should* look like. Because, in my estimation, society is often completely wrong; for example, I definitely don't want to do marriage the way I've been taught it should be. I don't see a lot of happy couples doing it the way you're "supposed" to. Generally speaking, tuning in to what we think things "should" be like is a recipe for unhappiness. I hope I will make that clear throughout these pages.

I've also been working through shame and vulnerability as I try to achieve intimacy in a way that feels right to me. But I also have to be able to bypass reflexive shame about failure in order to know when it's time to leave a situation. With every passing year, I've been learning more to listen to my intuition and trust myself. It's like I always know what's right for me, but sometimes I feel bad doing it so I hesitate longer than I should. So now, even if the world doesn't understand what I'm doing, I have learned to follow my gut. Even when I know it will be hard, and may cause someone to be hurt, myself included.

For me, sometimes the "work" has been identifying and dodging quicksand, by which I mean the relationships where I could easily have gotten stuck and then spent years of my life unhappy. Luckily, I'm not one to linger once I get clear on a decision. But if there's a thing I have learned from my work with couples, it's that many people would have stayed in places I left.

I can't say whether it's right or wrong, but I hope one of the outcomes of reading this is readers feeling empowered to realistically and honestly assess for themselves *whether* they should stay or go, using whatever criteria is right for you. As my favorite advice columnist Cheryl Strayed once wrote, "…*Go, even though there is nowhere to go. Go, even though you don't know exactly why you can't stay. Go, because you want to. Because wanting to leave is enough…"* (From her book, "Tiny Beautiful Things"). It doesn't have to make sense to anyone else.

I also spend a lot of time trying to understand, *"Why am I like this?"* and playing around with the answers I come up with, sorting and slotting and rejecting them as I try to build an answer that feels true. As we move through this, I invite you to think deeply about your early messaging about relationships and how that messaging informs how you do relationships as an adult. Getting clarity around *"why you are like this"* is important "root" work that many of you have probably not done, especially if you have not spent much time in therapy.

I'd like to state for the record that therapy is a great place to explore your roots, to take a close look at what formed you, and to encourage you to reject or embrace that early messaging depending on its current value and resonance. There are many paths to healing, and many ways to do this root work. Personally, I have been to seven different therapists and a number of alternative spiritual coaches and healers (which I jokingly refer to as "witch doctors") over the years, with varying degrees of success and insight achieved. I did some work around "healing my inner child." I've received Reiki/energy healing; I did past life regression under hypnosis twice. For one strange year, I regularly used a tarot reader as if she was a therapist.

I'm just saying, I've made my way through many different healing modalities and firmly believe you can find wisdom in all kinds of places and learn from all kinds of teachers. I did all that while concurrently staying present with my work, helping my clients navigate what they're going through, and learning from them as well. And it's still been quite a mess at times. In the end, I'd say all the experiences have been invaluable and "worth it" because all of it goes into the great big stewpot of healing work that's been brewing on my stove for 40 years. I feel quite certain I'll never be done growing and healing. It is likely you won't either.

Here are some questions you may want to ask yourself that stem from the work I've done for and with myself:

*What did your family of origin teach you about what relationships look like?*

*What did you learn about commitment and resilience?*

*What did you learn about dysfunction and co-dependence?*

*What did you learn about sex and intimacy?*

*What did you learn about communication and conflict resolution?*

*What did you learn about boundaries?*

Personally, I learned early that I generally lacked skills in the whole area of Relationship, probably in part due to my own family of origin. My parents divorced when I was 15, and it was a relief when they did, because they had co-existed in a space so full of tension for so long that it sometimes made it hard for me to breathe. To be fair, I doubt they knew they were affecting me in such a way, as I don't think it impacted my sister or brother in the same ways. I certainly didn't have the vocabulary as a child to fully express the discomfort I felt being in the house with them together. But my experience highlights that we must keep in mind that some children are very sensitive to the energy around them, and so "staying together for the children" can actually be quite harmful to kids, those empath kids in particular.

In couples' counseling sessions where there are children involved and divorce is on the table, I always disclose this information upfront when clarifying my position that I do not believe parents should stay together only for their children. I always explain that I personally believe that it didn't make any of our lives better to have my parents stay together so long. They stayed married 24 years, but from what I understand, only a handful of those were happy. In many ways, life is long, and so there is ostensibly time to figure things out, but I also believe it's too short to be willfully unhappy once you've identified that you are.

I'll talk more about this later, but it is my personal and professional opinion that children do better with happy parents, whatever that looks like. I feel like you should know this right away about me. This is my stance, provided separation and divorce are done respectfully, amicably, and with kindness. My parents did a good job with this, which also informs my belief that it can be done well.

On this note, a few years ago I completed the training required to be a mediator in my state because the idea of helping couples divorce peacefully appeals to me. The skills required for effective mediation are invaluable in my work. I still do counseling, not formal mediation, but that training gives me an expanded framework for thinking about how and why people end relationships, why so many struggle to do it well, and ways I can help them do it better.

Overall, I am a person who values relationships and finds them endlessly interesting and informative. While I do enjoy individual counseling, couples' counseling is my heart's work. As I've been working on this book, it's become more and more clear that I should be doing much more of it!

It's important to know that I believe any relationship that sincerely works for everyone involved can be accurately defined as "normal," *even if* you're the only ones doing it the way you're doing it. I also firmly believe in the idea that we are all here to live our best lives, to access and live into our highest selves, and to connect with and support one another.

I'm writing much of this during the pandemic of 2020; the shifts in the culture during this bizarre and unprecedented time may change how this book may otherwise have turned out. I am acutely aware of the ways in which we have been failing ourselves and each other. I don't know yet what will come of the COVID-19 crisis, but I already see that much will change, and rightfully so.

Obviously, I can't be your therapist or coach through a book, but I can offer you what I've learned from my personal and professional experiences. I believe that we cannot effectively engage in healthy relationships unless we have understanding of and access to our highest selves. Being clear on who you are and committed to living into the best version of yourself possible will aid you in creating the kind of intimacy you desire. That is the work I have been doing for myself, and I feel certain that I have finally landed in the relationship I am best at and which offers me the greatest chance for happiness; out of all the situations I've encountered, this is the best one. And I met him when I was 36, so I had plenty of time to kiss frogs, as it were.

It helps that I am the best version of myself in my early 40s that I've ever been, and I know that is the main contributing factor to why my marriage is working as well as it is. (It helps that my husband is very healthy and that he's a counselor himself!)

I am here to help you navigate your self-development as well as your relationships, whether they be intimate friendships, short or long-term romantic relationships, or even marriage. While I'm at it, I also wish to dispel the idea that marriage is some sort of perfect ideal to strive for. I want to suggest that it's just another stop along life's journey; it's neither the beginning nor the end. You can go there or not, and be just as happy either way. If you never get married, it means nothing about whether your life was a "success." Your life is *already* a success, and it can only get better from here as you add to your skills and insight.

I want you to be thinking about your own relationships, with your self and others, and to start taking a look at your patterns and the history of how you "show up" in your life. What are the questions you've been trying to answer? Take some time and get clear on what they are. Make a list. *(Seriously! It can be really powerful to see your stuff on paper.)* You can borrow my questions and answer those, or you may want to make up your own. (There are lots more to come, too.) It doesn't really matter what gets you started, I just want to encourage you to journey down this introspective path. In the next lesson we will get into some particulars, but this is one starting point: *"Why are you like this?"*

## Reflection:

*Have you ever done the root work I'm talking about? If not, what has kept you from going there? Are you ready to do it now?*

*How do you feel when you consider your relationship history?*

*What words would you use to describe your relationships thus far?*

# LESSON 2: WHO ARE YOU?

Now that I've introduced myself and explained the work I've done and am doing, and encouraged you to join me in that work, it's your turn. Some of you may find this section redundant because you have done a ton of work on yourself already, and that's great! But other readers are probably either therapy newbies or maybe even actively therapy-averse, which means you may not have ever really put much thought into some of this. That's okay, but it's time to do it now. I firmly believe that this work of understanding ourselves and cleaning up our own emotional houses is imperative to the later work of being in a healthy relationship with someone else.

I do want to be clear that nobody is perfect *(in fact, perfection isn't even a thing)*, and I don't think it's necessary to have everything figured out in order for you to be well-positioned to have a healthy, happy relationship. But I do think you need to have a reasonable amount of self-awareness and a willingness to unpack some of your issues, which we all have to varying degrees. You have to be committed to walk a path of growth, with the knowledge that you never actually "arrive" anywhere. You just keep growing and evolving and, with any luck, becoming an ever-better version of YOU.

The first step of that seems to be getting clear on who you are at your core. Like, your most authentic, reflexive, natural self. It sounds like a simple question, but when is the last time you explored it in depth and with a critical eye? Get out some paper and a pen and start making lists or drawing pictures or using whatever recording style works best for you. I want you to take an inventory of YOU. I invite you to be vulnerable, honest, and deeply intentional about this inventory. Answer some or all of the questions posed here. We'll call this a solo homework assignment, but if you're reading this with your partner, have them do the same thing and use your answers to share information with each other that you may not have before. Authenticity and a willingness to be real are both paramount here.

Speaking of "real"…I remember this moment so clearly, as it was pivotal for my thinking about relationships. I had a client a couple of years ago who was consistently upset because she felt like she didn't have meaningful connections in her life, and worse, didn't know how to form them. She asked me with tears in her eyes, *"Do you have a lot of friends? Do you have people you love and that love you?"*

At the time, I wrote this about it on my blog: Generally I try to not talk *too* much about myself, but sometimes use of self is very important to connection, so I said: *"Yes, I do have many people that I love and that love me."* But when she asked, *"But how do you do that?"* I wasn't really sure how to respond.

I guess I don't really know "how" I build such strong connections, because I've never really thought about it like that. Until fairly recently, I wasn't in the habit of thinking about relationships in such scientific terms at all.

What I told her was that I think my best and strongest relationships usually grow from the places I am being most consistently myself. I had to clarify that "myself" isn't always that great, and the fact that I'm clear on where I'm lacking or falling short is maybe even the most important factor.

She said she wants to be perceived as "having it all together." I laughed, gently, and told her I basically have *never* had it all together, but I'm okay with that, and actually I think that's probably why people like me. I think sometimes my semi-controlled chaos makes them feel like maybe we're all doing okay. I am very willing to be vulnerable in public.

I told her that nobody needs her to be perfect, because that's not even a thing anyway. I was like, *"I talk to a lot of people about their lives and I am certain nobody actually has it all together."* She was skeptical of this. She has a hard time being "herself" because she worries so much about being negatively evaluated that it seems to paralyze her into inaction. You can see how this is especially unfortunate when what she wants more than anything is to act courageously and reach out and connect.

All this talk made me think of *"The Velveteen Rabbit"* and being Real. I sent her my favorite quote from the book when I got home that night. I told her that if there *is* a trick, it seems mindful, positive, unselfconscious authenticity is the magic thing. I guess I intuitively already knew this, but to put it in words: the people I am most myself with are also the people who love me the best, presumably because when we (humans in general) live in alignment with who we are, especially who we are as our best and highest selves, most of us are actually pretty great.

It's only when I (we) start to shift and morph to fit whatever I think is expected that I don't feel connected like that, and it seems like any relationships I build from this place suffer from awkwardness or banality. Being a chameleon or trying too hard is exhausting to the spirit and is transparent to others, whether they are conscious of it or not. Basically, people probably won't like you if they think you're full of shit. I know it sounds trite to tell a client who's paying me good money, *"Just be yourself"* but there simply isn't better advice.

I know a lot of my clients struggle with this, and honestly, the greater your natural empathy and emotional intelligence, the greater your skill is likely to be at morphing and adapting. Being flexible and responsive to people is not *inherently* problematic. That said, issues do arise when you start to pay more attention to managing other people's perceptions of you than you do to just, like, existing. When you're watching every micro-expression on someone's face and shifting your responses accordingly, you're not being present in your body. It's work. It's exhausting to the spirit, even if you don't recognize it as such. And over time, it moves you further and further from your alignment point of "Real."

(That said, I would be remiss if I left it that at. Some people live their entire lives having to do this work for literal survival. It is a privilege to be able to drop all concern about how other people are receiving and responding to you, so if you're able to do that, I would invite you to appreciate it as the gift that it is. If you are not, I hope the world catches up to the notion that we all deserve this freedom, and that you nonetheless do your best to be fully and authentically YOU in the situations in which you are safe to do so.)

Anyway, I think what I decided from thinking through this with her is that the more authentically you can approach everyone you meet, the more Real you will seem to them. Yes, of course, people like to be flattered and affirmed, but when it comes down to it, people respond more favorably to authenticity. Generally speaking, I think people who are Real are valued more highly than people who pretend to be perfect. Don't even get me started on how much social media contributes to the perception that other people are doing life better than you, or are happier than you, or whatever. It's all bullshit. Nobody's life is perfect, I promise.

In my opinion, risking exposure through vulnerability is *where it's at*. Building healthy relationships requires honesty, authenticity, integrity, and loyalty. All that good stuff…but with a dose of *not being afraid to mess up*. Strong relationships are built intentionally by being courageous when challenged, and having difficult conversations, and inviting people to be Real with you back.

In sitting with this woman and hearing her express such a strong desire for those connections that I sometimes take for granted, I fully realized that is the best thing about my life. The relationships I have with the people I love are basically the only things that matters in my life; they are what sustain me and get me through all the other stuff. They help me to be Real. Where are you most Real?

*'It doesn't happen all at once,' said the Skin Horse. 'You become. It takes a long time. That's why it doesn't happen often to people who break easily, or have sharp edges, or who have to be carefully kept. Generally, by the time you are Real, most of your hair has been loved off, and your eyes drop out and you get loose in the joints and very shabby. But these things don't matter at all, because once you are Real you can't be ugly, except to people who don't understand."*
— Margery Williams, from "The Velveteen Rabbit"

In order to partner well, it is crucial that you are clear on what is most important to you, and you know who you are at your innermost core. You must be willing to be Real. If you find that being Real is a challenge for you, let's take a look at what might be getting in your way. The next few lessons may help you get some clarity.

There is no limit to the reflection you can do in this lesson. You can spend as much time as you need here before moving on. Maybe you've never done this work before, and it's revealing some surprising stuff. That's great! Maybe it's just reminding you of work you've previously done that needs a little upgrade and some new attention. Maybe it supports your impression that you're actually doing pretty well and are in tune with yourself. Whatever the case, it's here for you to use again and again, however you need to.

## Reflection:

*Where and with whom are you most "Real?"*

*If being Real is hard for you, what gets in your way?*

*Does the stuff about people-pleasing and micromanaging people's perception of you sound familiar? If so, does it feel like something you could or want to stop doing? What might that look like?*

# LESSON 3: VALUES

*What would you list as your "core values"?*

What I mean when I ask this: what are the things you hold to be true and right? What is important to you in how you move through the world and relate to others? What beliefs do you espouse and how do they align with how you live? Here is a non-exhaustive list of some things people might consider their core values, but please feel free to come up with your own:

- Authenticity
- Achievement
- Adventure
- Autonomy
- Balance
- Beauty
- Compassion
- Challenge
- Citizenship
- Community
- Competency
- Contribution
- Creativity
- Curiosity
- Determination

- Equity
- Fairness
- Faith
- Fame
- Freedom
- Friendships
- Fun
- Growth
- Happiness
- Honesty
- Humor
- Influence
- Inner Harmony
- Justice
- Kindness

- Knowledge
- Leadership
- Learning
- Love
- Loyalty
- Meaningful Work
- Openness
- Optimism
- Peace
- Pleasure
- Popularity
- Recognition
- Religion

- Respecting Authority
- Responsibility
- Rules
- Security
- Self-Respect
- Service
- Spirituality
- Stability
- Success
- Status
- Trustworthiness
- Wealth
- Wisdom

*Once you have your core values listed, the next step is to ask which of said values are authentically, truly yours (i.e., in alignment with your truest self) and which are inherited, whether from your family of origin, society, or both?*

*Of the values that aren't authentically yours, which might you reject if you were being totally truthful with yourself? What kind of courage might it take to reject these values? Do you feel like you need "permission" to change? Can you give yourself that permission?*

Here is an example from my own life: I am older and wiser now and quite unbothered by grammar mistakes and spelling errors, but for the first 35 or so years of my life, I was known for being rather pedantic about such things. I thought it was totally okay to be snarky about people not knowing the difference between "your" and "you're," for example. *(I cringe while sharing this, by the way. It's so classist and gross, but I've committed to being vulnerable with you, so I am.)*

So in making my list, a few years ago I might have said that I have core values of "Valuing Education" or "Following the Rules" or (less generously) "Being Right" or "Not Making Mistakes."

At some point in the past few years, I started reflecting on "my own" versus "inherited" values. I began to realize that pedantry was something I'd identified early on as a quality that was rewarded in my family of origin, and also by the circles of society I moved in. Being snobbish about grammar allowed me to declare a position of intellectual superiority and it signaled that I had achieved some higher education because I was "above" certain foibles. (I thought it did, anyway.)

This attitude I held was deeply ingrained in me, and required some intentional excavation to remove. At some point I decided that being classist or snobbish wasn't congruent with who I am at my core, and certainly not in alignment with my highest self and who I want to be. Generally speaking, I have since stopped responding to the innocent mistakes of others. I may still notice errors *(and will feel embarrassed if this goes to publishing with any errors!)* but I'm now able to notice without judgment. My current belief is that communication is communication is communication. If people can understand you, and you're not writing for publishing, do it how you want. This feels like growth, but, more importantly, it feels like it's in alignment with my highest and best self.

So in naming the shift, I could now say some of my core values might be "Valuing Communication In All Forms" or "Offering Grace" or something neutral-to-positive like that. Do you see how this shift is important? I still have the same ability to notice errors, and I still value education and precision with language, but I removed the need to make any of it mean something negative about a person making a mistake. I removed the piece that relied on someone else's mistake to make me feel superior, because "feeling superior" pushes me out of alignment. Make sense?

The mission here isn't just to pick apart your value system. It's also not only about identifying your own values, but it's also about doing the work of critiquing your inherited values and measuring their alignment with who you truly are and who you want to be.

So, referring to my example, perhaps you can find places in your own life where you have adopted or lived into values that, upon deeper analysis, are not *(quite or at all)* in alignment with your best, highest, and most authentic self. The first step is to identify and name them; the next is to find ways to reject and replace them with values that do align with who you want to be. Spend as much time on this as you need. We all have a lot of old stuff that doesn't fit anymore; this practice is about piecing together a value system that is intentional and current. You may have to do this work multiple times in your life; we have all received a great deal of bad programming.

A client recently used an analogy I love (and wish I'd come up with myself.) He said basically that we all are born with a garden space. Society and our families start planting in our garden the day we're born, and so all kinds of shit gets planted in it before we're even old enough to realize it. As adults, then, our work is to tend to that garden and uproot everything we didn't agree to have growing there. That weeding work is what this particular lesson is all about. Weed out what doesn't belong in your garden, even if your family or the culture doesn't get why you don't want it there.

At some point, the goal is to look around your garden and be able to identify everything you've got growing there. Make sure everything in your garden is there on purpose. Then the key to long-term happiness is to do the everyday work of tending to your garden, weeding, watering, and keeping it healthy. And moving forward, only planting things in it that you want to grow.

If you're currently partnered, you may want to talk with your partner about their values, share yours, and compare them. See where you align with each other and where you may not. Get curious about each other. What is growing in each of your gardens? Ask lots of questions. Talk about whether compromises or shifts can be made or whether you both believe the difference in values can still mean you live harmoniously.

## Reflection:

*When you look at your values, are you surprised?*

*Are you living in alignment? If not, how much work will it take to shift your life into alignment with your core values?*

*Why do you think it's so common for people to adopt or live into values that aren't consistent with who they truly are?*

# LESSON 4: FEARS

I don't know about you, but fear steers my ship far too often. I have a tendency toward anxiety anyway, and in these anxious times, I'm finding it more and more necessary to tune in to and critically examine my fears. I am trying to be more consciously aware of when fear has too much power in my life, and to evaluate when it's reasonable to be afraid and when I'm having an anxiety attack.

Fear is an adaptive response to real or perceived danger, and throughout the course of human history, it has served us well. It was decidedly useful to fear and be prepared for attack from neighboring tribes, dangerous wild animals, or whatever dangers lurked. But in modern day-to-day life, there's not *typically* a great need for hyper-vigilance or excessive fear. *(There are plenty of obvious exceptions: living in an area with a great deal of gun violence, being in an abusive situation, living during a pandemic, etc.)*

Assuming the places you live and work are reasonably safe, if you're regularly living with too much fear or anxiety it is crucial that you get whatever help you need to reduce it. Chronic anxiety can significantly decrease the joy you are able to access on a regular basis. It's stressful on your nervous system; it can disrupt your sleep, make it harder to stay present in your relationships, and it puts you at risk of addictive behaviors.

Personally, I really don't want to live with anxiety as a baseline state, and I find that clients with anxiety are equally eager to try things that might help them feel better. Anxiety disorders are on the rise right now, so it's a good idea to find a therapist who specializes in them if you're finding that none of your usual tricks are helping. Some of the things I do that help me include: avoiding caffeine, soaking in Epsom salt baths, taking CBD oil, and sleeping with a weighted blanket. But you may need more than this; I strongly encourage you to find a skilled therapist to give you tips and tools to help you manage your anxiety.

When it comes to more general fears (unrelated to an anxiety disorder), I have learned to tune in to my fears and give them name. I find that naming my fears helps me to "declaw" them, as it were. Contrary to popular belief, it doesn't make them any more real, and it doesn't make them more likely to be "called into" your life. It does, however, take a certain degree of courage to name and face your fears, especially deep ones with strong roots.

With clients who live with a lot of fear, I often use the analogy of fear being a passenger in your car. So I might say something like: *"Okay, let's not let fear drive the car. Let's start with simply asking it to scoot over into the passenger seat. It's still there, maybe annoying you by fiddling with the radio or talking too much, but it's not ruling things. You can still go where you intend to go. Over time, you can banish it to the backseat and eventually it can drift out the window and leave you to drive in peace. At that point, you can go anywhere!"*

It may sound silly, but most people respond well to metaphor. Personifying your fear or worry as an unwanted passenger can be a useful way to think about it. That said, if you have another analogy or way of thinking about it that works better for you, by all means, do it your way. The goal is to be aware of our fear and when we are allowing it too much power.

So let's take a fear inventory: *What are your greatest fears?*

I don't mean phobias like spiders or snakes or heights, although for the sake of sharing with your partner, feel free to list those too. I am thinking more about fears related to life and how you live. Fears like, *"I am afraid I won't find someone to love"* or *"I am afraid of being hurt again"* or *"I am afraid of losing my security"* or *"I am afraid everyone will find out how afraid I am."* This sort of thing. Existential fears. The kind of stuff we don't usually talk about or acknowledge. The vulnerable stuff that keeps us up at night. Make a list; most of us have many of these fears.

For example, a deep old fear of mine is that I'm not good enough, just sort of generally. This manifests in a variety of ways, one of them being wondering in some nebulous way if I even deserve to be loved. Now, it's important to note that I am consciously certain of the love my husband holds for me, but this fear is real nonetheless. If I don't keep an eye on it, it can trickle into my relationship dynamics in the form of needing to be reassured regularly that I am loved. I may go to great lengths to get this reassurance. I may do it in roundabout or passive-aggressive ways. And, it's important to note: it's annoying and frustrating to both of us when I do this.

More importantly, it is cyclical and will come back again and again if I don't do something different. So my work is to name it, own it, and release it. Over and over, I tell this fear to fuck off. I remind myself that I'm not unlovable. No matter how many times my inner child whispers or shouts it at me, it is not true and *I know it's not.*

So one thing I do regularly is affirm myself, and so I offer this affirmation to you as well: *"You are more than enough, and you are loved and lovable."* A spiritual coach and mentor encouraged me to add, *"But more importantly, you will be okay no matter what."*

This is a value of mine, and you can think about whether it resonates with you as well. I believe it is vitally important that I try to manage my own fears, fill my own cup, and not require (too much) external validation in order to feel good. This is a practice, and it's challenging, and I work on it regularly. When I feel my old fears creeping up, I check in with myself and adjust in whatever ways I need to. If it's a reemergence of clinical-ly-concerning anxiety, I call my therapist and make an appointment. If I've slacked on my self-care and I can manage my feelings by working out more or getting more sleep, I recommit to those practices. If there's a conversation my husband and I need to have, we have it.

As for our relationship, it is crucial that my husband knows and understands my fear stories so that he can be sure not to activate them unknowingly. Make sure your partner and anyone close to you is conscious of the things that trigger your anxiety, so they can make a good faith effort not to cause you harm.

I want to be sure to acknowledge that depending on your cultural background and lived experiences, you may have different kinds of *very real* fears than someone else might have. Those are also important to identify, understand, and discuss with your partner, particularly if your partner is from a different culture or background than you are.

For example, I understand a great deal more about the common (and completely justified) fears of Black Americans than I might otherwise, because my husband shares his fears with me. If he didn't, even with the best of intentions, I might not fully grasp the degree to which the fears of Black Americans differ dramatically from the fears I'm personally familiar with from my own lived experiences.

The best way to learn about others' lived experiences is through connecting with them and offering them safe space. The intimacy and trust of sharing fear stories is a crucial element in how we can be known to each other in profound ways. This principle certainly applies to other relationships besides intimate partnerships. It can build connection, understanding, and empathy in all our relationships.

When exploring fear stories with each other, remember that while curiosity and even ignorance are acceptable, you *don't* get to tell someone else that their fears are unfounded or silly. This is especially relevant if their life experiences have been quite different from yours; just because you can't personally imagine it doesn't mean it isn't real.

As such, you must refrain from arguing, gaslighting, or attempting to justify, even if your feelings get activated. Comparing fear stories can be powerful, but it only works in the absence of shame and judgment. If the conversation lends itself to discussion about your reaction to the sharing of fear stories, all the better for connection and understanding. I'm a big fan of communication about all the things. Just make sure you don't co-opt the sharing, get defensive, or make it feel unsafe for others to share their stories, as that would defeat the whole purpose of the exercise.

For yourself, try challenging your fears by naming them, objectively evaluating the case you've built for them, and rejecting them if you find they are unfounded. Replace these unfounded fears with accurate and hopeful information. *"I can't open up because I am afraid of being hurt"* can be replaced with something like, *"I recognize that I am afraid, but I know I am resilient and can handle what comes my way. Fear is not a good reason to avoid love. I deserve to be loved and I understand that with great love comes great risk, and I accept that risk."* Talking to your fears can be powerful. Assessing the actual risks involved is useful, since you may find you're worrying about something with very little evidence. You may not even realize the extent to which fear is driving your car. It's an incredible sense of freedom to let it glide out the open window on the highway, even if you have to crack that window again and again and again. The work is worth it.

## Reflection:

*What is the story behind your fears? Do you know where they come from? Again, interrogate their roots: are they your own fears or do they relate to something passed on to you from your family of origin or the greater society?*

*Do you have evidence for the validity of your fears?*

*Have they served you in some way?* Sometimes we hold on to fears for longer than they serve us because we are convinced that avoiding scary things keeps us safe.


*Is it time to outgrow or challenge some of your fears? What might happen if you did?* Name potentially positive and negative outcomes. Then evaluate whether it's worth doing the work.

# LESSON 5: BLIND SPOTS
## AND OLD HABITS

A literal blind spot is "an area in which view is obstructed," so when I refer to blind spots in counseling work, I mean those areas where you either lack knowledge or the conscious access to insight. Your view is obstructed, for whatever reason. Most of us have blind spots, often around areas of privilege like gender or race. But this could really refer to anything you routinely act on without awareness. It could be triggers from childhood you don't realize you have. Blind spots are often a result of the way you're socialized, both in your families of origin as well as the broader society.

Regardless of their origin, the frustrating thing about blind spots is just how hard it is to see what you're doing in an objective light. So you may be acting in *conscious* good faith, meaning you *think* you are doing good or right things, but your lack of vision doesn't allow you to actually see yourself clearly, much less make progress. In other words, you don't know what you don't know.

Blind spots may be glaringly visible to others. They could account for those negative or critical things your partner, family members, or friends have pointed out to you, perhaps many times. You may not like to hear these things, but that doesn't discount there could be a pattern. Maybe you have historically refused to acknowledge your blind spot(s) or perhaps you get very defensive about them. You may know there's a whole world out there you can't see, but it feels like everyone else can.

It's okay to be scared to acknowledge these things, but it's powerful to change them once you're ready. It is healthy and wise to invite feedback on your blind spots so that you can get to know yourself fully. You may have noticed that the current political climate is placing the blind spots of many people in the spotlight. You may be frustrated with the conversations you're having with relatives or friends where you can clearly see their blind spots, but they steadfastly refuse to acknowledge them. That is frustrating, but perhaps will be useful to remind you that you probably *also* have those. With the understanding comes an obligation to try to highlight, examine, and work on them.

You've heard the adage "old habits die hard," right? That's so real. Old habits in this case could more aptly be referred to as "bad habits." I'm talking about the messy maladaptive stuff we do to protect ourselves, which often shows up in the form of poor reaction and over-reaction. These are habits that you hold on to even when you see that they aren't serving you anymore, or maybe never did. You just may not know how to interrupt them.

Examples of bad habits that show up in relationships include: yelling, name-calling, gaslighting, deflecting, stonewalling, or retreating. Maybe you do some mix of all of those. It is very common to have habits like this, so don't be too hard on yourself or shame spiral if you read this and it stings. It is very likely that you don't know how to replace these old habits with new ones just yet. Maybe you've tried but so far you always seem to revert to your old ways. It will require diligence and compassion with yourself, so get ready.

One practice is this: ask the people you're in relationship with to give you feedback about your blind spots and bad habits. Ask them to be extremely honest with you. Mine for answers to questions about what it's like to be in relationship with you. You may want to say something like, *"What are some behaviors I use that get in the way of our relationship?"* Or *"How can I show up differently in this relationship that might feel better to you?"* Or *"Are there some areas that I need to work on that you've been afraid to tell me about?"*

In order to encourage people to feel comfortable responding, you may want to add something like, *"I am ready to hear those things now, and I will do my best to not react defensively. If I do, however, please know that it's my own stuff getting in my way, and you didn't do anything wrong."*

Be sincerely open to receiving their feedback and incorporating their suggestions. This may require significant effort and courage, because when you give people the opportunity, they may really let you have it. It kind of depends on the quality of your connections, how well they feel you've treated them, and how long they've been holding on to the feedback. Hopefully they'll deliver their thoughts and feelings with kindness, but regardless, this is probably information that will help you grow.

If the feedback stings, step away and spend some time with those feelings. Do your best not to be upset with them or make the other person feel like it was unsafe to do what you asked them to do, especially if you did add the caveat I suggested. Additionally, remember that this feedback is for your growth, so try to *only* use it for that purpose. Do not use it to shame spiral, confirm a suspicion you have about yourself or your relationships that you already know is going to feel really bad, or feed any negative self-talk.

Seriously: if you read all of this and it sounds like you're not ready to do this work yet, skip it for now. Don't do anything that is going to make things worse for you overall. But if you think you can and will use any feedback productively to make some much-needed positive changes, then proceed.

Another useful practice is to notice who seems to not have quite as many blind spots and bad habits as most of us, and ask them, *"How do you do that?"* Find out what their practices are. What healing work have they done? What do they do for self-care? How do they stay healthy? What do their self-talk loops sound like? It is helpful when possible to surround yourself with and

33

emulate people who are healthy and/or who are committed to actively working on themselves in a loving and compassionate way. When the people around you are healthy, it's easier for you to prioritize your own health.

And, of course, this is where I'll gently remind you that you may want to go to therapy if you have unresolved issues, blind spots, and old habits that you have a hard time getting a handle on. If they are getting in the way of living into your best self, prioritize working on them. *(By the way, most of us do have some of these.)* Or if you got the feedback and want to change, but feel paralyzed when it comes to starting the work. This is where therapy is super useful, because you get to focus exclusively on YOU and what you want to work on and get better at. Your therapist is on your team and wants to help you succeed and be happy. You'll be better at all your relationships if you get clearer on your blind spots and work on shifting your old habits into new and better ones.

As for the overall arc of this book, remember that while you do not have to be perfectly put-together to have a good and easy*ish* relationship, it certainly can't hurt to be the best and healthiest version of yourself. A worthwhile goal is to get to a place where you can see yourself clearly and consistently feel good about what you see. It is useful to have someone else hold up a mirror and show you what you don't or can't readily see on your own. It can be painful, but it's worth it. Sometimes you need assistance to be able to really dig in and do some radical self-reflection and growth.

## Reflection:

*Do you have a tendency to repeat the same mistakes and/or get the same negative outcomes over and over?*

*What are some of your "old/bad habits" that you know aren't serving you?*

*What feedback have you gotten from others in your life about things they wish you would either do or not do? What has kept you from shifting?*

*Is there something you know you're avoiding that, if you were to shine light on it, would make a huge positive difference?*

# LESSON 6: HOW TO FIND A THERAPIST

It occurs to me that throughout this book, I have and will continue to recommend that you go to therapy, so I should probably give you some concrete advice on how to actually do that. I should not assume that everyone even knows where to start!

First things first, let me be perfectly honest: *it can be challenging to find a good therapist who's the right fit for you.* You have to be prepared to shop around, and to move on from a therapist who isn't a good fit, without getting discouraged. In full disclosure, I've seen seven different therapists over the years!

That said, I can give you some tips that might help you find a counselor that is a good fit for you. It can only help to have someone with real expertise on your team to assist you as you work through some of the challenges in your life, including some tough questions that may arise as a result of reading this book. Growth isn't easy! Build a support team that includes a therapist and a few "trusted advisors." Your trusted advisors may be friends, colleagues, or family members; it doesn't matter. Just make sure they're people you trust to offer wisdom and honest feedback when you need it.

The next big thing to consider when shopping for a therapist is insurance and fees. I would strongly advise against going to someone *just* because they accept your insurance, if you have some flexibility there. Of course, I understand the desire to use medical insurance, and even the need for it. *I'm not saying don't use your insurance!* I'm just saying don't make it the *only* deciding factor, if possible. There are a few considerations to be aware of around using medical insurance for counseling.

One thing is that when you use your insurance, you have to get a medically reimbursable diagnosis. What that means is your therapist has to give you a diagnosis that the insurance company has agreed warrants them paying for treatment. Having a diagnosis on your health records isn't as big of a deal in the age of the Affordable Care Act (aka "Obamacare") since you can't be denied coverage due to preexisting conditions. However, given the current political situation as of this writing, I have some concerns about the viability of this provision in the future. Even if this provision remains, you'll probably still want to be aware every time something gets added to your health record. So if you use your insurance to pay for counseling, you can be certain you're getting a diagnosis of some kind.

Some therapists may not explicitly state this. I didn't know it until I joined my first private practice in 2012 and the practice accepted basically all insurance plans. Anytime we billed a client's insurance, I had to give them a diagnostic code. Prior to that, I had willingly and happily used my own insurance with my first therapist because it made it cheaper for me, but to this day I have no idea what she diagnosed me with. I didn't know to ask! She would have had to provide some kind of evidence for the diagnosis, whatever it was. Just know that if you're curious, you have every right to ask your therapist what they are diagnosing you with if you go this route.

Another consideration about insurance is this: if you have a high deductible to meet, you may end up paying the same amount out of pocket that you'd pay either way, or maybe more, until you meet your deductible. So if you're not going to meet your deductible in a calendar year, it may not make much difference to your financial bottom line whether your therapist bills your insurance or you pay them directly and bypass insurance. It is important to note, however, that if you use your insurance, you won't pay the therapist's private pay rate; rather, you'll pay the amount they've contracted with your insurance company to charge their clients. So it probably would still be cheaper to do it this way unless the therapist has a reduced fee rate they offer for people choosing not to use insurance (or who don't have insurance).

If you're in a different situation and have great coverage, a low deductible, and/or have met your medical deductible for the year already and therefore your total amount due to the therapist is a relatively low co-pay, well, that's obviously a compelling reason to prioritize finding someone who accepts it. It also makes a lot of practical sense to use your insurance if you have a diagnosis that requires the monitoring of medication, a lot of interfacing with psychiatrists, and/or may require coverage like in-patient or intensive out-patient treatment.

That said, many good therapists don't take insurance, myself included, so you are seriously limiting your options by only looking at therapists who do *if* you have options. I get it if you actually can't afford therapy without your insurance, in which case I am really glad you have it! Just look into it fully and don't just assume you can't, especially if you find a therapist you really like who doesn't accept your insurance. Explore all possibilities and ask a lot of questions.

Some might argue that it's classist to not accept insurance, an argument which I would completely understand. I think it totally *is* classist, and renders therapy effectively out of reach for millions of people if a therapist does not offer a sliding or reduced fee option to offset the often-prohibitively-expensive private pay rates.

Since beginning my own practice, I have always offered a reduced rate option. It's important to note that I have almost never had anyone ask who didn't need it. Generally speaking, people are fine to pay the full rate if they can, and will only ask to reduce it if they can't. I accept their request without asking for proof. That said, be aware that some therapists will ask for tax records or some other demonstration of need; this is fairly standard practice, so don't be offended if they do.

Also, your insurance plan may offer out-of-network reimbursement, so you may be able to recoup part of the fees if your therapist doesn't take insurance but is willing to give you a diagnostic code and a "superbill" to submit to your insurance company. Call your insurance company and see if you have out-of-network coverage. These days, this is less common than it used to be, but some plans do still have it.

Another option is to contact a local graduate school counseling department and make an appointment to see an intern; typically these sessions are very low cost or free. Provisionally licensed counselors may also have low cost or free sessions as they work towards their licensure hours. Just because a therapist is new or still learning doesn't mean they aren't good! While clinical skills and experience are important, being a good therapist is largely about relating to your clients and having solid interpersonal skills, which often come naturally to folks predisposed to do this work.

So yes, certainly, therapy *can* be expensive. However, it can be contextualized as a long-term investment. The significant increase in your productivity and happiness is the "return on investment" that you'll get if you stick with it long enough to reap the benefits. As for frequency, that's up to you. Lots of people prefer weekly or biweekly sessions. But going once a month is better than zero times a month, so do what works for you.

Many people are legitimately struggling, especially right now, but in my experience during non-pandemic times, some people will use, *"I can't afford it"* to more accurately mean, *"This doesn't seem to be worth what it is going to cost"* or *"I can't imagine spending that much on myself and my mental health so I'm going to just deal with this stuff on my own."*

The fact that you are actively thinking you might need or want to talk to someone is a clear indicator that you really should, so please figure it out if you can. If you find someone you feel safe and comfortable with and stick with it a while, you'll feel better. It's not *exactly* magic, but it absolutely does work if you commit to doing it and have a good connection with your therapist!

Next, in terms of *how* to pick a counselor, the easiest thing to do is to ask your personal network who they have seen. Don't just go to someone your friend or co-worker used without some due diligence, but do look them up and see whether they feel good to you. If they do, reach out to them; all the better that they've been vetted by your friend. Word-of-mouth referrals are the bread and butter of a thriving therapy business. I'm super grateful for all the referrals I've gotten over the years.

Another thing you can do is use the search engine offered by Psychology Today (or some other therapist search engine) and look at a whole lot of profiles. If you use the PT search, you can sort by criteria that is important to you *(e.g., race, gender, location, insurance, area of expertise, modality, fees)*. Save the ones you want to come back to in an ongoing list. Look at all of their websites in depth. If they have blogs, read them. Try to get to know them that way and to get a sense of what their style is.

Along those lines: trust your intuition. If someone's website feels good to you, or you think they look nice or kind or warm or something nebulous like that, it's not crazy to use that as information in your decision-making. Personally, every medical provider I've ever really liked I chose based on this question: do I like their face? *(Obviously they also have to have the credentials required, but all other things being equal, liking their face helps me decide.)*

With this, you may be afraid you're deciding something so important based on something intangible and potentially non-rational, but honestly, you have to like the way your therapist's face looks. They have to feel good to you. This may sound shallow, but it's not. I don't mean they have to be "attractive," I just mean you have to find their face pleasant to look at. You have to like their vibe. You have to *like them as a person.* You're going to be telling this person all of your innermost thoughts and feelings, so feeling safe and comfortable and "liking" them is crucial.

This is important because evidence consistently shows that the therapeutic relationship is *the most important factor in healing.* The connection between you and your therapist is a hugely significant part of what makes you get better, or not. Seriously. A counselor can have all the technical skills, education, and experience in the world, but if they don't deeply connect as a human being with their clients, all of that is basically useless.

It's as simple as this: you have to like me, and I have to like you, or it won't work as well. For me personally, that is another major reason I don't accept insurance; the people who choose me do so intentionally, not because I was on a list somewhere or because I was cheap for them to try. They did their research and determined before we began the work that I might be a good fit for them, which saves a lot of time in the long run. They are usually intuitively right about our goodness-of-fit when they choose me organically.

I know this whole lesson is a bit of a departure from the rest of the book, but I think it is important to pause and give you this guidance. (Personally I don't mind a tangent, but I know some readers prefer things to be more linear.)

The bottom line is this: *therapy does work.* And yes, I know it's expensive, in terms of both money and time. I know it's a big commitment. I know it's vulnerable, and I know you may be reluctant (or even afraid) to tell a stranger all your business. I get all of that, but I promise when you find the right fit, therapy is really wonderful. When you're a good fit, it really is the connection with the therapist that helps you start to feel better.

Because, think about it, when's the last time you had someone on your team who was there just for you? What I have seen over and over is that you can really start to blossom when you have someone who's squarely in your life, who accepts you fully and regards you positively, unconditionally...but will also tell you when you're messing up. This is someone whose feelings you don't have to manage. A great thing about this relationship is it is not reciprocal, in that you don't have to care about your therapist the way you care about a friend or family member. You don't have to think about whether you're talking too much or being self-centered. In fact, that's kind of the whole point.

You literally don't owe your therapist anything except payment and presence and a willingness to be vulnerable. Their job is to pay attention to you, validate you, challenge you, and invite you to see yourself and your situation in a different and better light. They have knowledge and expertise they want to offer that will help you feel better. Doesn't that sound awesome?

## Reflection:

*What has your experience of therapy been?*

*If you haven't been to therapy, what gets in your way?*

*What would you hope to get from therapy, if you were to find someone who was a good fit?*

# LESSON 7: SHAME

*"Shame is a soul-eating emotion."* — C.G. Jung

O kay, now we're back to regularly scheduled programming. Let's talk about shame. I hadn't really put much thought into shame until I facilitated a three-part group series a few years ago called *"Shame, Vulnerability, and Intimacy."* It was pretty incredible. I had so many people sign up that I had to split the groups and have two concurrent groups going on alternating weekends. Who knew so many people were ready to talk about this stuff? It was cool because all the participants deeply connected with the ideas and each other, and were willing to be open and share. A lot of growth came out of it, including for me as the facilitator.

My theory going in was that shame is often *the thing* that gets in the way, even without us recognizing or naming it as such. Without resolving shame, we would always struggle with vulnerability and find true intimacy nearly impossible. The group process confirmed my theory. We started with shame and were able to identify a number of areas where people are likely to experience shame:

- Who you are as a person *(i.e., just feeling a fundamental shame that pervades everything)*
- Something that happened to you *(e.g., abuse or trauma)*

- What you've done in the past *(e.g., spending time in prison, risky behaviors, bad decisions)*
- Sexuality and gender *(e.g., orientation or non-conformity)*
- Sexuality *(e.g., desire, kink, type of sex)*
- Religious *(e.g., sin, shame around sex)*
- Body *(e.g., feeling too _____ or not enough _____)*
- STD diagnosis *(i.e., something avoidable but permanent)*
- Addiction
- White privilege/white guilt
- Socioeconomics *(e.g., growing up poor)*
- Low social status *(e.g., women, LGBT, BIPOC)*
- Food *(e.g., over-eating, restricting, food shame)*
- Masculinity *(e.g., not feeling like a "man" or being shamed for some perceived weakness or femininity)*

This list is definitely not exhaustive; *what are some we missed that you can think of?*

I'll just say it: shame is the worst feeling. I remember the last time I found myself in the midst of a gut-wrenching shame cycle. I had taken my own advice about not making assumptions, asking hard questions, and vulnerability. I had reached out to someone I was pretty sure was avoiding me. I learned from her response, because she used her words and told me, that I'd disappointed her. I'd hurt her and left her feeling abandoned when she needed me.

I didn't get defensive. I couldn't. She was right! I didn't realize I'd done something at the time, but when she explained her side, I could see why she felt that way. And I felt terrible about it. All I could do was apologize and ask how I could make it right. That's what I would tell any client or friend to do in a situation just like this one.

I would say, *"Own your shit, apologize sincerely, ask how you can mend the damage, and then move on in the direction of the answer."* Or I might say, *"Don't feel bad beyond a reasonable amount of remorse. Guilt and shame are not useful"* Or maybe I'd say, *"You're fine. Everybody makes mistakes. Learn from it, make amends, and don't do the thing again."*

I know all the things I would say, and I said them to myself. Yet that ashamed feeling lingered. That feeling of being vaguely "in trouble," but like, instead of with that specific person, I was in trouble with life itself and my worthiness to it.

I don't want to project, but I'm guessing many of you know the feeling. It's so dramatic to describe, but there's that moment when you discover you've done something wrong or made a mistake, and the next thing you know you've descended into a spiral of *"I'm the worst...I don't deserve good things... nobody loves me...I should just give up...I suck at life"*...etc, ad nauseam, until it either organically passes or you (I) get some clarity and distance.

*(In my case, it was the latter this time. But I actually know from working with some of you that it doesn't pass easily for you. So maybe this will help.)*

The thing about these shame cycles: not only do they not really help you do better, they actually cripple you. They stop you in your tracks. They barricade you from vulnerability. Shame floods you with false assurances about your *fundamental ain't-shit-ness*. It encourages you to wallow in bad feelings when instead, what's happening could be a profound lesson for you. Instead of wasting time feeling like a piece of garbage, you could be taking inventory of what you need to work on or clarify or be mindful of. As I've said a million times, feelings are not facts. And shame is just a feeling, albeit an extremely convincing and awful one.

To clarify, shame is a step beyond guilt. Guilt, according to Brené Brown's definitions, is feeling bad about *what you did.* Shame is feeling bad about *who you are.*

I would invite you to start with just recognizing your shame cues, because until I started doing this work on purpose, I had never really identified what the feeling even was. I just knew I hated when it happened.

Think about it: *What happens in your body? Can you imagine and name it?* For me, it's a rush of warmth to my face and instant nausea to my belly. It feels like panic at first, and then it settles into a low hum of near-constant anxiety until it passes. I can't eat or sleep when I'm in this state. It feels like anxiety, but with an added edge to it. Again, it took me years to understand what the feeling is and be able to name it, so don't feel bad if you haven't gotten there yet. It might take a while to be able to tune in.

But once you know how the feeling of shame shows up in your body, you can start to recognize it right away. Here is the next practice for you: begin paying attention to the situations or people in your life that trigger you to feel ashamed. It may be happening way more frequently than you realize. Conversely, you may find that it is only occasional but that it tends to linger.

Whatever the case may be for you, next time you find yourself starting to spiral down the emotional trash chute that is a shame cycle, use all your will to pump the brakes. Go check in with someone you love and trust and be like, *"I really screwed up, am I still okay?"* and they'll say, *"Yes,"* and then hopefully you can breathe a little bit, give yourself some grace, and handle your business from a clearer place.

What I don't want you to do is turn inward, keep it all to yourself, and continue the spiral. It is important to check in with someone because you may need that external grounding and reassurance before you will allow yourself to stop spiraling. *Shame requires secrecy to flourish.* As soon as you say the thing you are ashamed of out loud, it loses some of its power. Especially when someone you love is able to say, *"It's okay. I still love you."*

I keep mentioning Brené Brown, but she really is the expert on this stuff, and I'd be remiss if I didn't credit her. She said something that has stuck with me since the first time I heard it, and which has fundamentally shifted how I react when someone shares something they feel shameful about. It's this simple: *"Empathy is the antidote to shame."* When you feel ashamed, what you mostly need is empathy. You need to know you're not alone, and that someone else hears and understands you without judgment. Likewise, when someone else feels ashamed, what you should strive to offer them first and foremost is empathy.

Fred Rogers once said, *"Anything that's human is mentionable, and anything that is mentionable can be more manageable. When we can talk about our feelings, they become less overwhelming, less upsetting, and less scary. The people we trust with that important talk can help us know that we are not alone."* In other words, empathy is the key to unlocking shame.

Looking onward, what if we not only avoid the paralysis of a shame spiral, but we were able to pretty immediately translate these experiences into learning tools? Does that feel possible to you? For me, it does, even though it's challenging.

Once I moved through the incident with the friend I mentioned and was able to hear and understand how I'd disappointed her, I was able to name specific things I learned from it. I'm glad I was brave enough to ask if she was upset with me and hear the answer, because I'm always trying to improve how I relate to the world and the people in it. And based on what she said, it's clear I needed to receive the feedback. Obviously I wish I had been a better friend to her in the first place, but once I messed up I just wish I had been better at bypassing that soul-eating shame on the way to the clarity I eventually received. I'm going to keep working on this, and I hope you will, too. It's worthwhile work.

## Reflection:

*What role does shame play in your life? What do you feel ashamed of?*

*What are your shame triggers?*

*What are some of the things you tell yourself when you're shame-spiraling? Are you able to interrupt the spiral?*

*What does shame feel like in your body?*

*Prior to now, what would you have identified those feelings as? Does it change anything to now call it "shame?"*

# LESSON 8: VULNERABILITY AND HEARTBREAK

*"To love at all is to be vulnerable. Love anything and your heart will be wrung and possibly broken. If you want to make sure of keeping it intact you must give it to no one, not even an animal. Wrap it carefully round with hobbies and little luxuries; avoid all entanglements. Lock it up safe in the casket or coffin of your selfishness. But in that casket, safe, dark, motionless, airless, it will change. It will not be broken; it will become unbreakable, impenetrable, irredeemable. To love is to be vulnerable."*
— C.S. Lewis, "The Four Loves"

The next step in that class series was vulnerability, and I want to acknowledge upfront that vulnerability is really damn hard.

Full Stop.

When we talk about vulnerability, we inevitably also talk about broken hearts. Much of what you are doing when you avoid vulnerability, whether consciously or not, is trying to avoid heartbreak and pain.

I was talking with a client the other day, and she said she has never gotten over her first real heartbreak. She described how it influences and interrupts all of her other relationships, often before they even begin. I can relate. Maybe you can too.

My very first real relationship was when I was 21. I was so in love with this person, who also happened to be the first woman I'd been with, and I was truly vulnerable for the very first time. Prior to this, it had always been extremely hard for me to talk about my feelings *at all*. I used to write a lot of sad and dramatic poetry, but when it came to saying actual words out loud, I couldn't do it. I don't know why. Anyone who knows me now might find this hard to believe, but it was like I had a lock on my mouth and I just could not break it open to say anything that would make me the slightest bit vulnerable.

So it was a big deal that I was madly in love and completely willing to be vulnerable with this woman, because I had to work so hard to achieve that state. To her credit, she also worked really hard to get me there. It was intense and profound. And so when she ended the relationship abruptly, I was beyond devastated. I couldn't eat, I couldn't sleep, and I barely went to class. I'm lucky I graduated college; I was paralyzed with grief and sadness and...anger? Regret? I think those were the real residual feelings, which related directly to the vulnerability I'd agreed to experience, and which had decidedly not paid off. I felt betrayed. I remember feeling like, *"What the hell is this?! You said this was safe. You promised."*

What I didn't know at the time was that *she* wasn't ready for vulnerability; it was even more terrifying for her than it was for me. I was at least willing to go there. She really wasn't, but she wasn't able to communicate that fear to me. The lock on her ability to express herself did not have any key I was able to find, and the relationship couldn't survive my trying.

Once the relationship ended, in the absence of information, I turned it all inward. I blamed myself for everything, which of course was wildly unfair, but I didn't know better at the time.

All told, I think it may have taken me a full six years to recover from that heartbreak. I may still not be recovered, if I'm being all the way honest. I certainly still struggle with vulnerability; it's just that I'm more willing to do it anyway. At my age now, I believe and accept that it is absolutely imperative to experience vulnerability in order to have real relationships. I know with certainty that true intimacy requires vulnerability.

But that doesn't make it less scary. I don't recover well or quickly when deeply hurt, and so there is always fear mixed in with the relief and joy vulnerability brings. There is always the ghost of that very first heartbreak lurking around, reminding me in vague whispers that I could lose everything I love at any time. I'm sure I have some reflexive emotional responses that relate to this experience. We are cumulative, after all; we all carry all of our stuff with us.

But I always return to the idea that you can't really, truly appreciate the good stuff without going through some of this terrible, heart-breaking stuff too. Had I never had that relationship, I might not have known what it felt like to be laid bare to a person, and to experience profound connection. Who knows if someone else would have been able to do quite what that specific person did at that specific point in my life? I think I needed that entire experience, despite how painful it was when it ended.

Sometimes it does seem to take getting deeply hurt to catalyze change. Sometimes we have to be forced to shed our old skin in order to re-grow and be ready, be better, for the next person who wants to love us. I certainly wish that weren't the case, of course, because who wants to be hurt? But until we all get better at all of this *(gestures broadly)* it will probably continue to be true, and we will just have to be brave and do our best.

That woman who broke my heart and I are real, actual friends now, almost 20 years later. I visit her city about once a year and we spend a couple of days catching up and then go the rest of the year with very little contact, and it's all okay. We're both in better places now, and we've both done a lot of healing work. Like all the rest of my hard-won life lessons, I wouldn't change any of it. It was all part of my story, and in many ways, it readied me for later relationships.

I do know that a lot of people go through their whole lives never feeling what I felt at age 21, and that makes me sad. That feeling was profound. It cracked me open, changed me, and left me ultimately better off. I needed that to happen. And it's like I have the grown up version of that radically vulnerable, deeply connected relationship now with my husband, and I'm so grateful for it. I choose to believe that early heartbreak and everything else I have experienced had to happen in order for me to be able to fully open to and appreciate this.

Many people spend their whole lives "avoiding entanglements," and finding other, non-emotional ways to spend their time and energy. I know a lot of you reading this would probably rather stay safe than take big emotional risks, especially if you experienced profound loss early on. I understand the desire to protect yourself. And yes, if you keep your heart locked away, you will (ostensibly) remain unhurt. But in holding yourself back, you will also be untouched, unchallenged, and unmoved, which to me seems worse somehow.

*To love is to be vulnerable.*

If you have children, you know how true this is at a core level. That's a different dynamic, of course, but the truth is that the more you love someone, the greater the risks involved. The more it would hurt to lose that person, or that relationship, the scarier it can feel. But I'd invite you to always remember that as much as it sucks to be hurt, heartbroken, betrayed, and all the other miserable possible outcomes, there is always the equal chance of connection, partnership, understanding, deep and abiding love. To me, that seems worth the risk vulnerability presents. What do you think?

## Reflection:

*What are your experiences of vulnerability and heartbreak?*

*Have they been worth it, now that you've lived the outcomes?*

*Has the trajectory of your life made it easier or harder to be vulnerable?*

*How does intimacy relate to vulnerability, for you? Can you have one without the other?*

# LESSON 9: VULNERABILITY AND HAPPINESS

*A ship is safe in harbor, but that's not what ships are for."* —John A. Shedd

Look, there's a pandemic happening as we speak. As such, I have had a lot of time to think. And I have been thinking about courage, risk, alignment, doing what you love, being with people you love, being authentic, and what I really want my life to look like. And how to advise others to get their lives where they want them to be. And how to help all of us to just be happy, but not passively. Happy in an active and dynamic way that is open to changing direction as needed. Happy in a way that is attuned to your inner guidance. Happy in a way that invites intimacy and radical connection. Happy in a way that is realistic and sustainable.

Quick question: *What do you think of when you think of happiness, for you?*

It seems to me that active happiness and true intimacy require risk-taking and vulnerability. Yes, the dreaded V word again. I have so much more to say about it. Let's call this lesson Vulnerability Again Because It's Super Important.

Fun fact: I have an ex who would literally call it that *("the V word")* because I hated it so much I didn't like to say it or even hear it. It made me so uncomfortable that the very *word* felt awkward in my mouth. She thought it was funny and weird that I couldn't say the word, but honestly it was a real problem for me.

I can at least say the word now, so suffice it to say, I've come a long way since then. But if you hate the V word too, I don't blame you a bit. It's basically the worst, but as I stated in the previous lesson, I have learned that it's also the best. Moreover, it's entirely necessary. But it's still hard and so it's something I work on every day, in many different forms. Here is how I think of vulnerability and what I mean when I use it in this book and in my work:

- Vulnerability is extending yourself without assurance that the outcome will be desirable.

- Vulnerability is asking for what you want despite the fact there's a chance you won't receive it.

- Vulnerability is deciding to make a big change because the status quo of your current situation is just not making you happy.

- Vulnerability requires courage and faith in your ability to navigate new territory.

- Vulnerability is the most direct route to true intimacy and connection.

- Vulnerability requires a willingness to possibly fail, but more importantly, a willingness to accept a bigger, better life for yourself.

Hint: *You have to believe you deserve it.*

You have to position yourself to receive the good stuff life is offering, even if the shift into receptive positioning is scary or involves risk. It seems to me that pushing off from the safe harbor is key sometimes, and until you do it, you can't expect more than *this* (whatever *this* looks like for you). And it can be really scary. You may have what Brené Brown calls a "Vulnerability

Hangover" after a profound moment with the V word, and it may be intensely uncomfortable. Honestly, anytime you take a big risk it's natural to feel nervous. It's worth it, though, and I promise it gets easier the more you practice.

In order to consistently live in a state of active happiness, you will need to get comfortable with the fact that nothing is certain, vulnerability is required, and risks are necessary. You have only this day guaranteed, and so you are charged with making the most of it. You can't just sit idly by and hope that good things come your way. You will have to venture out and make changes happen.

To some extent, you have the power to manifest your own outcomes. Within reason, of course, I mean, you're probably not going to magically "manifest" a million dollars or meet the love of your life just by having a thought about it. But the first step to active happiness is being able to visualize yourself having the kind of life you want. A vision board is actually great for this because it's useful to be able to see your dreams in front of you. You will have to be ready to work to make your vision a reality. But most importantly, *you have to believe in its existence.*

You have to push off from the safe harbor. Wasting away in safe harbors is not what we are for. We are for sailing. We are for active happiness.

## Reflection:

*What issue(s) or habit(s) are you holding on to because the alternative is more scary than this familiar thing? In other words, what keeps you stuck in the harbor?*

*What does "active happiness" mean to you?*

*What steps might you need to take to get from where you currently are to a state of sustained "active happiness"?*

*What happens if you try and fail?*

# LESSON 10: STRENGTHS AND JOYS

*"When you do things from your soul, you feel a river moving in you, a joy."*
— Rumi

I t is important that we not dwell too much in the negative, as it's easy sometimes to just get overwhelmed by all the improvements you think you need to make. While that's crucial work, it is just as necessary to get super clear on the amazing and wonderful things about you and how you're showing up in the world. I am positive that there are many wonderful things about each of you! Being aware and celebratory of the ways in which you are uniquely qualified to bless the world is an asset that can't be overstated. I'll spend a lot of time focused on work you need to do, but please spend some of your reflection time answering these sorts of questions too, the ones that affirm and celebrate you.

## Reflection:

*What brings you the most joy? What can you do to cultivate more joy in your life?*

*Where and with whom do you feel the most joyful and authentic?*

*What are you great at?*

*What accomplishment(s) in your life are you the most proud of?*

*What do you bring to the world that no one else does?*

*What are the attributes you love the most about yourself?*

*How do you want to be seen by your person? Does it align with how you actually "show up" for them?*

# LESSON 11: LOVING YOURSELF

*"I celebrate myself, and sing myself."* — Walt Whitman

I will continue to reiterate how crucial it is that you consciously work toward a goal of loving and accepting yourself fully, even in the process of growth. Be your own first love. Give yourself the gift of your own grace. Celebrate yourself. The world is lucky to have you! It is so, so important that you know this.

First, in case no one has told you yet today, please allow me: *You are beautiful.* You are amazing and wonderful and smart and kind, but especially you are beautiful. I say that twice not because how you look is actually that much more important, but because *you* may believe that it is. And so I want to tell you that I know in my bones that there is nothing wrong with you or your body or how you look. You are just fine how you are right now, today. You know why? Because you are YOU.

When I find myself lamenting how I look in some capacity, like maybe I've gained weight because it's hard to get motivated to exercise during a pandemic, or my hair isn't how I like it, or I just feel gross today, my husband always shrugs and says, *"To me, you just look like Amy."* Without fail, that is his response. Even when I look super extra cute and I come strutting out in my fancy heels, with full makeup and fake eyelashes on, and am like, *"How do I look?"*…he *still* says I just look like me. He is basically unmoved by any changes in my appearance, even ones I might think are dramatic. It used to bother me until I realized the gift it is. What he's saying when he repeats this isn't, *"I don't see you."* Instead, he is saying, *"I do see you, but I also see you every day. And I love you regardless of how you look from day to day because, to me, you are always the same person I married and still adore."* Which is pretty awesome, actually.

I am trying to learn from him. And so this is the approach I try to take with myself. I try to remember that I am always me, every day, all day. I am me at any weight and any hair style and any amount of makeup. I am the same me as I age and sag. In our culture, it's easy to forget that who you are isn't what your face or body looks like. The face and body are just a shell for your person, or your soul, or your essence, or however you think of it.

So you should know that in reality, no amount of makeup, exercise, weight loss, weight gain, new clothes, hairdo, beard shape, braces, or even surgery is going to make you any more or less *you*.

## P.S. THIS IS TRUE FOR WOMEN, MEN, AND GENDER NONBINARY FOLKS ALIKE.

Much of what we're doing when we strive for physical perfection of some sort (whatever we think of it as) is trying to escape ourselves and/or improve ourselves from the outside in. That's not how any of this really works. Who we are starts from the inside and shows itself on the outside.

If you're an awful person, no amount of external beauty is going to make up for that, despite what celebrity culture would have you believe. In the real world, having good thoughts, being generally happy, defaulting to kindness, and having an awareness of the other people in the world all make us more attractive and appealing *to the kind of people worth having relationships with*.

Most importantly, however, believing you are worthy of love *as you are* and insisting on being treated as such is what demonstrates your value to others. In large measure, you teach people how to treat you based on how you treat yourself. That doesn't mean they won't test or try you, so this also includes showing them where you draw your boundaries, so they know what you won't tolerate. This is why I always stress that having solid boundaries is a gift and not a problem.

The truth is, people who really, truly love *you* aren't going to love you more if you lose ten or even a hundred pounds, and people who were never going to love you right no matter what you do don't get a vote on anything. If someone's love for you is contingent upon you maintaining a certain appearance, then their love is conditional in a way that makes it hard to believe in.

I'm certain this is a phenomenon you'll encounter regardless because our culture is really screwed up in a lot of ways; this obsession with diets and thinness is one of them. A friend once told me that when they got married, her husband informed her in no uncertain terms that if she got fat, their marriage was over. WTF, right? She thought it was funny. She apparently agreed to his terms, and married him. It's not my place to tell her that I think her husband is a real jerk for saying that, and also, I do believe that if a relationship makes both parties happy, it's "healthy," so I kept my opinion to myself.

However, if that had been my to-be husband, I think I'd be like, *"Well I can't promise you anything, but if your love depends on me looking a certain way, it's not the kind of love I want."* Because even if my intentions are to always maintain a healthy weight, there is no guarantee that life is going to always go the way I plan. Personally, I would encourage you to look for the kind of love that says, *"You are always you, and I love you for YOU."*

Now, I will say that it may be true that possessing a strong and healthy body makes it *easier* to have a happy heart and a joyful spirit. You may be more able to approach life with some degree of consistent optimism. Being able to move around comfortably in your body makes it easier to feel good in your soul. It is a thing to be wildly grateful for if this freedom in your body is your current reality. And so I will also say that paying deep attention to the actual health of your body, not whatever fad diet or unattainable beauty standard we're trying to live into these days, may emotionally prepare you for exchanging the kind of love you want. It is important to learn how to treat yourself well and show care and compassion for yourself.

That said, there is *not* a direct causal link, and I need you to believe me. Losing weight or changing your body in some way will not make you more lovable or more deserving of love (which you already are). It won't magically bring you the love of your life. It literally won't do anything beyond make your body potentially healthier and more comfortable for you to live in. So it might make *you* feel better so that you are more open to being loved, and that I can get on board with.

I just want us all to get clear about what our intentions are when we "work on our bodies" and make sure we're coming from a positive place and not a self-loathing or critical place. Diet culture is incredibly harmful and extremely profitable. The beauty industry makes a ton of money off our collective insecurities; you can imagine that all of this messaging about how you're not good enough just how you are makes it really hard to live in a healthy and happy relationship with your body.

Our absurd cultural beauty standards indoctrinate you from birth with the idea that you cannot be happy unless you are constantly bullying your body into meeting those impossible standards. Instead of embracing our differences and celebrating that we're all beautiful in our own ways, and can be beautiful and healthy in many shapes and sizes, it can make anyone who isn't <perfect by these rigid standards> feel like they can never fit in.

But guess what? It seems to me that people who've managed to opt-out of the fight are consistently happier and healthier than those who are still engaged in it. Learning to live in peace with your body and to treat it well is imperative for healthy, happy living *(and eventual partnership, since it's hard to accept love if you don't believe you fundamentally deserve it).*

Lest you mistake me for saying, *"Don't care at all about your body's wellbeing,"* I want to reiterate that it is true that maintaining a healthy weight may very well factor in to your overall physical well-being and the way you feel in your body, and that once again: that's a conversation worth having! But I'm here to remind you that, at the end of the day, nothing (no thing) about your body impacts your intrinsic value as a human being, one way or the other. Being "thin" doesn't necessarily mean you're healthy, it just means you're thin, which holds no moral advantage over any other body type.

So! In order to be the best version of yourself and to ready yourself to welcome a relationship hallmarked by (relative) ease, I'd invite you to get started or continue the work to be easy*ish* in your skin. This body is the only one you have, and life is more peaceful when you are kind to it and able to live harmoniously.

If, like many of us, you've received a lifetime of critical messaging (from yourself, the culture, and maybe other people) about your body, this can mean there's a lot to unpack. Don't stress if this is a tough lesson for you and it takes a long time. I'm in my early 40s, and I'd say I'm just now getting here. So be patient with yourself, but know that kindness towards yourself and ease in your skin are definite assets when it comes to relaxing into and trusting the intimacy of a serious relationship.

**Reflection:**

*When you think about the points I'm making here, what comes up for you? Does this feel inspiring or depressing? If the latter, what shifts might you need to make?*

*How does it feel to think about "loving yourself"?*

*Are you historically hard on yourself? Where does it come from?*

# LESSON 12: NEGATIVE SELF-TALK

*"Putting yourself down is easy. Out minds are built for self-abuse. The work is in lifting yourself up, giving energy to the many ways in which you are strong and beautiful and so very worthy. Just as you are. It's easy to hate yourself. Why not effort at loving yourself, each day, with your thoughts, spoken words, and actions. To love yourself is the most important work you can do."* —Scott Stabile

So now I have offered my perspective on loving yourself in your body and hopefully you've had a chance to reflect on it. You may have determined you're not quite there yet. That is completely okay, and I'll keep saying that at every step. It's all a process, and some of these lessons will feel easier than others. But this is crucial, soul-deep work. This work is about getting to deeply know, trust, honor, and love yourself so that you are crystal clear on what kind of relationship you want and deserve, with yourself and other people. I saw a meme about self-talk a few years ago that stuck with me. It read, *"It's hard to be happy when someone's being mean to you all the time."* WHEW. That is a word, isn't it? When you find yourself saying cruel things to yourself, I'd invite you to recall this sentiment.

Always remember that the best way to position yourself for a healthy and successful long-term relationship is to make sure you are intact. Build yourself up until you are a whole person. Ensure that you've done your work sufficiently so that you always recognize yourself as lovable and worthy. Even if the world didn't give you this messaging nearly often enough throughout your life, you can take charge of your healing at any stage and change the story. I know it isn't easy, but this is of utmost importance.

It occurs to me often in the course of my work as a counselor that the hardest person for many of us to actively love is ourselves. So if you're struggling here, I understand and you're in good company. My guess is, if you're like most people, you can be unspeakably cruel to yourself at times. You likely talk to yourself in ways you would never talk to anyone else. It is crucial work to monitor your self-talk loops, and interrupt them when you start saying mean things. You may be surprised by how often you have to do this, once you get into the habit of tuning in.

It makes sense how you got here, but it's really important that you heal this relationship you have with yourself and begin being kinder. It's hard because you receive so much negative messaging, often starting with your families of origin. That happens even in the healthiest of families, so multiply that tenfold if your family is dysfunctional. Negative messaging can also come from your religious background, from being bullied in school, or from someone you've been in relationship with. Many of you have been abused by others in myriad ways, making it easier for you to erroneously believe you deserve to be treated badly.

Some of you were raised by people who failed to treat you with the unconditional love that all children need and deserve from their parents and primary caregivers. I want to tell you sincerely that I am *so sorry* you did not get what you needed at this crucial point in your life, because you absolutely did and do deserve to receive it. *It was 100% not your fault that you did not.*

I would be remiss if I didn't say that, because it's possible you truly don't know how much this may have affected you in adulthood. When you do not receive that early safe and secure attachment in childhood, you may grow into an adult who is naturally mistrustful and suspicious of others. Or you may grow into an adult who is willing to accept scraps of "love" because you don't know what it feels like to be truly safe and accepted in relationships, or maybe you simply don't believe you deserve better. But you should know: *you deserve better.*

Let me say this plainly: your parent(s) or caregiver(s) failed you. Maybe they tried, or maybe they didn't. Maybe it wasn't their fault. Regardless, whether you can (or choose to) empathize and forgive them for it depends on your specific situation and your temperament. But whatever happened to get in the way, it absolutely was their job to love you unconditionally and offer you secure attachment. Their failing to do so, for any reason, *does not reflect on your value or worthiness.*

It does, however, mean you may struggle with attachment as an adult, which may show up in your relationships over and over despite your best efforts. Please know that there are therapists specifically trained in attachment issues who can help you repair this loss you sustained in your formative years. This is work worth doing.

Some of you may carry around the fear that if someone -anyone- really knew you, or knew all the things you had done, they could never love you. You may not even be able to name where they originated, but for whatever reason, your feelings of shame have convinced you that you do not deserve to be deeply known and loved.

Some of you live with a nebulous but ever-present certainty that you are simply and organically not deserving of love. Again, you may not even know why or where this belief comes from. But in this case, too, hear me say this: it is not true. You are worthy. Every single person reading this, please know that I fully believe this: you are absolutely and entirely deserving of respect, belonging, safety, and love. You deserve this from yourself and from other people. The world needs you. You are deserving of all of the good things, right now, as you are, in this very moment. There is nothing you could do or say that would convince me otherwise.

This is a social work concept called "unconditional positive regard." It is a commitment I make to my clients. It's like: I accept your humanity and affirm your place in the world, regardless of whatever measure of "deserving" the world may apply. You are worth my positive regard at all times, even when I disagree with your actions or when you have made a mistake.

Now think about your own self-talk. Are you treating yourself with unconditional positive regard? Are you forgiving yourself for your mistakes and offering yourself grace? I am certain many of you reading this right now are not. In fact, some of you have probably criticized yourself multiple times in the process of reading this, because despite my admonishments to be easy with yourself, it may be dredging up all sorts of negative or anxious feelings. You may be feeling like you're doing life all wrong or worrying that you will never be happy.

Look, it's not that I have some secret information. I simply have the privilege of getting to deeply know enough people in my work and personal life that I can reasonably extrapolate what the general populace is doing. And so I am quite sure that many of you are actively being harmful to yourselves in this way, every day.

It could be the terrible things you say to yourself when your dress from last year doesn't fit or the *"You can never do anything right"* mantra that plays in your mind when your partner makes a comment that hurts your feelings or your boss criticizes you at work or when you're just having a bad day. Maybe you struggle with depression or anxiety and some days you treat it like a moral failing and are mean to yourself when symptoms creep in.

It could be the desperate fear of not being able to provide for your family in the ways you hope to, or the crippling sense of responsibility and the certainty of failure that follows behind it. As I'm writing this during a global pandemic, I suspect more and more of you are feeling this pressure and being even harder on yourselves. *(If I'm being honest, I'm feeling an urgency in writing this just to have another potential revenue stream given the uncertainty of the future.)*

Regardless of their source, I want you to reflect on all those things you say to yourself, and literally write them down. It's like the opposite of positive affirmations. It doesn't feel good. But seriously, write down all the hateful stuff you say to yourself, so that you can see in writing the abuse cycle you're in. More importantly, so you can see the abuse cycle you are in *with yourself*.

That's right: this mean voice is in your own head, and so essentially you are abusing your own self. Now, I do know that much of the time, the voice we hear is tinged with someone else's voice, most often a critical parent. That is a tough one because it sounds like it's external, and it's so old and familiar that it feels like it must be true. But it's important to remember that it is YOU who is saying it now. And this old nasty stuff you say to yourself robs you of confidence, keeps you small, and makes you afraid to make mistakes. It is crucial that you figure out ways to stop this self-talk loop.

Note: if this lesson is resonating with you, it's probably going to be painful work. You've been at this a long time and you're expert-level. But it's really important work once you're ready to fully commit to stopping the cycle. You are the only one who can interrupt it. This isn't work someone else can do for you, although per usual, a good therapist can help.

There is a lot of fear energy circulating through our culture right now; it is even more important that we temper our fears with kindness towards ourselves so that we can be brave and bold enough to get through all of this. So I'm going to challenge you to try radical self-love. It begins with being aware of your negative self-talk, and instead of defaulting to it, beginning to treat yourself how you'd treat a beloved friend.

Here is a practice: think of a dear friend whom you love. Picture their face.

Okay. So presumably, you endeavor to treat your friends with respect, kindness, grace, and forgiveness, right? You allow them space to make mistakes. You support them through the consequences of their questionable decisions. You don't savor their failures; you celebrate their successes and encourage them to persevere. You show up for them when they need you, without judgment.

And yet…my guess is you often treat yourself in almost the opposite way. You may expect yourself to be perfect, with unimpeachable actions, behaviors, and decisions. You may hold grudges against yourself when you make mistakes, and withhold forgiveness as though you are undeserving of grace.

In doing so, you refuse to allow yourself the joy and freedom that radical, unconditional self-love and acceptance offers. Even worse, you may retreat from opportunities for vulnerability and connection in the fear that you won't be good enough or measure up in some vague way. You may believe yourself to be fundamentally unworthy of your own forgiveness and grace.

But why, though? Real question: *Why are you doing this?* Why are you holding yourself to standards you expressly believe are unreasonable? You don't do this to others. You don't expect perfection of your friends and loved ones. (If you do, that is a thing to work on in tandem…)

Spend some time observing how you talk to yourself. And next time you find yourself thinking terrible, mean things about yourself, berating and self-flagellating, try to imagine addressing those very same words to the dear friend you pictured a moment ago.

I would venture a guess that you would never do this. You would never say those horrible things to them. And why is that? Because, I think, you know in your bones that nobody deserves to be talked to this way, but especially someone you actively love and care for. It would hurt their feelings and maybe make them cry. So then ask yourself this: why do you think you deserve to be talked to that way, if your friend doesn't?

The answer is: You don't. *You deserve unconditional positive regard from yourself.* So put this on your list of stuff to work on!

# Reflection:

*What is the most challenging aspect of this lesson for you?*

*When you look at your list of negative self-talk, what stands out to you?*

*Is it clear to you where your negative self-talk loops originate?*

*Do you hear your own voice or someone else's when you're being critical of yourself?*

# LESSON 13: WHAT DO YOU WANT?

A nother part of knowing yourself is being able to articulate what is most important to you when you are in a relationship. Get clear on what you want so that you can be intentional and deliberate in how you build your next relationship, or how you rebuild your current one to make it a bit easier.

I invite you to use this lesson to help you get clear on the kind of relationship you're looking for, who and how you want to be in the context of a relationship, and what kind of person you want to be with. It is also an opportunity to evaluate how prepared you are for the kind of relationship you're naming. If you find you are not prepared, it's totally fine. It just tells you that this is part of your work. And if you're in a relationship currently, you could do this lesson with your partner and see where you align and where you may not.

**Ask yourself (or each other) the following questions:**

*What aspects of yourself do you most appreciate when you're involved with another person? Do you always "show up" the way you intend?*

*What qualities do you hope your partner appreciates in you? How can you make sure you're bringing those best parts forward all the time?*

*What qualities do you most admire, appreciate, or desire in a partner?*

*When you think about a relationship being "relatively easy," what stands out to you as the hallmarks?*

*What kind of relationship would offer you the best chance at success and happiness? Is it the kind of relationship you have or have had in the past, or will you have to make some changes?*

For example, do you prefer monogamy or is some less conventional relationship more your speed? Just a little heads up: we really push monogamy in our culture, but it's not right for everyone. I will talk more about this later, but I just want to plant the seed that your best work will include investigating all ideas with rigor, regularly asking *"who am I and what do I want?"* This investigation will certainly include ideas that may be outside your current comfort zone.

*What are your dealbreakers?*

Make a list of the things you totally can't deal with or absolutely must have. I'll address my thoughts about such things in the lesson about compatibility, but for now, include your current ideas about dealbreakers in your inventory.

*How do you communicate and what is your preference for how others communicate with you?*

For example, some people are internal processors and need a lot of time to figure things out on your own; some of you need to talk everything out. Some people ask a lot of questions, but some people prefer to let the information unfold. There's no "wrong" way to communicate, so long as you are putting in sincere effort, but there are definitely easier and more challenging styles in terms of compatibility and ease!

Make sure you're clear on and can name your style and preferences, so that you can articulate them to another person. It's really helpful to know this at the beginning of a relationship, when possible, so I'd suggest you offer something like, *"I prefer to talk everything out, so make sure you let me know if there are times you're not in an emotional space to process with me.*" Or "*It can take me a while to figure out how I feel, but I'll come to you when I'm ready to talk.*" Or "*I like when people ask me questions to help me work through things.*" Or whatever applies to you. If you're currently in a relationship where communication seems to be a struggle, naming your preferences may help ease some of that struggle.

*If or when you find yourself daydreaming about the "perfect" partner, what do you think about? How different are they from the one you have, if you're already partnered? If you're not partnered, does this wishlist feel realistic?*

This is definitely a thing that people do: set themselves up to fail by insisting that the person who's right for them be this magical, perfect "The One" who meets all the criteria on their list. But looking for a cookie cutter perfect person is a surefire recipe for unhappiness. No one will ever be perfect. Perfection, whether in a person or relationship, is not a thing.

However, if we're talking about finding someone who is perfect *for you* in the ways in which their imperfections manifest, who has complementary strengths and weaknesses, and is therefore compatible with the ways in which you are equally imperfect...well, that's totally doable. Let's shift to a focus on discovering that complementary person instead of a perfect one so that we don't co-create our own disappointment.

The key here is getting to know what you want in a relationship, so that when you find yourself dating or meeting people, you are clear in your intentions. It is useful to be able to name your preferences, style, desires, and concerns. It is also helpful when you understand yourself well enough to know where you can be flexible and where you draw the line. Spend time on this lesson if it's not work you've done before. Some of us just fall into relationships and never examine how or if they align with what we truly desire or would find satisfying and (relatively) easy. Now's your chance.

# Reflection:

*When you were going through this lesson and answering the questions along the way, what new or surprising thing did you learn about yourself?*

*If you're currently partnered and you haven't answered these questions for each other yet, how do you think it might be helpful moving forward?*

# LESSON 14: PHYSICAL TOUCH AND OTHER LOVE LANGUAGES

*What is your love language(s)? How do you like to give and receive love?*

Gary Chapman wrote a book naming what he calls *"The 5 Love Languages®,"* and many people find its theories useful. In full disclosure, I don't often recommend the book itself to clients because it's faith-based (Christian) and that's incongruent with my practice, but I do tell my clients about the theory and reference it if they're into it. I always give credit to the author and suggest they look into it further if they feel called to do so. I do find the basic premises useful, regardless of one's religious perspective.

The gist is that we all have predicable and consistent ways that we prefer to have love expressed and that we prefer to express our love, which he names as follows: *Words of Affirmation, Acts of Service, Quality Time, Physical Touch, and Gifts.* Sometimes, the way we express and the way we receive are not the same. Sometimes our partner's preferences are the opposite of ours. This may sound confusing, so I'll offer a detailed example of how it could play out. This will also serve as a little lesson in how keeping communication lines open is crucial!

Let's say someone's preferred love language is what Chapman names "Physical Touch." Please note that this does not necessarily equal sex, although for some people it can and does.

*(Side note: I do wonder if that's partly because some of us haven't learned how to be sweet, tender, or expressive in other ways? Many men, for example, would probably cite this as their preferred love language, but then their partners complain that it primarily manifests as a desire for closeness through sex. I suppose that's another conversation altogether, but it's something to be thinking about. Like, why is sex the easiest/best/ most accessible way for many men to express love, but they struggle to express it in other physical ways? Often we see that they can express tenderness and gentle touch with their children but are uncomfortable being affectionate elsewhere.)*

The Love Language Chapman calls "physical touch" can encompass everything physical or affectionate, from a hug to a kiss to a pat on the arm to massage to cuddling to stroking your partner's neck or smacking their butt when you walk by. That said, it doesn't necessarily require any PDA or that you are constantly touching. It just has to do with making regular physical contact as a primary way to show affection.

This is decidedly not my preferred love language, but it is my husband's, so I have come to understand it better in practice. Remember: your love language describes how you prefer or are most easily or naturally able to receive and/or give love. My primary love language is "Words of Affirmation," so my cup is filled by praise and verbal appreciation.

It is important for those of us for whom physical touch isn't a top priority to remember that sometimes we can accommodate our partner's need for this by simply *being available and amenable to being touched*. For some people, doing the touching is sufficient, whereas some need the touch reciprocated, in which case we need to make a conscious effort to be more affectionate if this isn't our natural state.

If you are partnered with someone for whom this is a preferred way to transmit love, talk about it with them. Do not assume what this means, make sure you *ask* them how best to communicate physical touch to them. *Do they have a high sex drive or can cuddling or hugging meet the same need? Do they feel hurt or unloved if you don't routinely express yourself in a physical way? Would they like you to do more small gestures of touch?*

Think about how you respond to your partner's need for touch. *Do you pull away or get annoyed when they reach for you? Do you routinely tell them "not now" or "don't touch me" or "why are you bothering me?" without realizing that you're essentially turning down an offering of love? Does thinking about it in these terms shift anything for you?*

I intentionally mention this particular love language because I think sometimes we get into the rhythms and habits of our lives and we forget to tune in to being physical with each other, regardless of preferred love language. Connecting physically is an important element of an intimate relationship for most people. Sadly, I see lots of couples' affection that has withered over time, largely due to lack of expressed kindness through touch.

As a compounding factor, which I can now vouch for from personal experience, once you have children, you get touched (and climbed on and tugged on and demanded of), constantly. This is particularly true in the early years of parenting, which is often when couples report the earliest signs of disconnect.

Particularly for those of you who prefer introversion, this over-touching by the children can make being touched *more* feel burdensome. You may just want space and time to yourself when you don't have the kids near you. To be clear, it makes perfect sense that you might feel this way. However, you absolutely have to say words and discuss these feelings with your partner. You cannot assume they know and understand without you explaining it, and you *especially* cannot assume they don't take it personally. They may feel rejected, but rather than tell you about it, they may begin withholding from you as a way of protecting themselves. You can see how without lots of communication about it, couples may stop touching at all for reasons that aren't actually about the quality of the relationship.

Whatever the initial reason, if you don't talk about it early in the childrearing years, you may stop having sex, may stop being sweet with each other, and may shift focus entirely onto the kids. This can happen slowly, over time, and sometimes it takes a while before you really notice. Sometimes you're three kids in before you stop to wonder what happened. Ask yourself this now: when was the last time you and your partner just stood in the kitchen embracing, or held hands on the couch while watching a tiny bit of TV before dropping off to sleep? When was the last time you touched your partner's arm gently when you passed them in the hallway during the chaos of bath and bedtime for the little ones? Letting these small gestures of affection wither and eventually die off entirely is a recipe for disaster in the long-term health of the relationship. Even if the kids are happy. Even if you're still super affectionate with them.

So what can you do if this is your situation? Start by naming it and talking about it. It's not necessarily too late to start mindfully reintroducing physical touch back into the relationship. That might actually ease a lot of the other stressors that may have cropped up between you.

There are four other love languages that Gary Chapman goes into in his work, and I do recommend thinking about it, talking with your person, and finding a way to apply the ideas. Don't worry if you aren't quite sure which one appeals most to you; this isn't an exact science, so the question of, *"Well, what if I like to give it this way but I want to get it this way?"* doesn't really matter, of course. You can have whatever idiosyncratic style of love-transmission you want, so long as you're able to name and explain it to your person.

Seriously, your way doesn't need to fit one of Chapman's five categories. What matters is that you (and your partner) figure out and *effectively communicate* the specific ways you prefer to be treated, and give each other cues to recognize when the other is offering you love in a way that might not be natural for you or may not feel good to you. Name *your* love language, personality type, temperament, communication style, and so on, in whatever way you can. Always include as much data as possible in how you think about who you are, what you want, and what works for you.

# Reflection:

*What is your personality type? Or, what do you know about your personality and temperament that is pretty steady and consistent that you could describe to another person?*

*What are the patterns you see in your attraction to others? Are you routinely attracted to the same types of people?*

*Does this seem to have positive or negative connotations for your life?*

*Rank your love languages in order of most to least important, using either Chapman's suggested styles or naming them however you'd like. Is your current situation responsive to your preferences?*

*Think about your past partners or ask your present partner about their personality type, temperament, and/or love languages. How might it be or might have been helpful to know this information?*

*How do you think this could impact your relationships moving forward?*

# LESSON 15: NEVER SETTLE

I wish I could shout this from the rooftops: Never settle for less than you want, need, and deserve when it comes to love. Never knowingly agree to live out of alignment. Don't waste too much time in a relationship that isn't meeting your needs, lest you begin to forget that you have needs at all, especially if there are clear signs early on that things are not likely to change. Remember that while people are absolutely capable of (even very dramatic) behavioral changes, they *fundamentally are who they are.* So never allow yourself to ignore things that are consistently true about another person.

Example, if someone is emotionally unavailable right now, and you know it, you cannot be surprised if and when that person continues to be emotionally unavailable. Whether you choose to move forward with that person or not is up to you, but you have the information and therefore are equally responsible if the outcome is undesirable.

If someone is emotionally damaged in such a way that it renders them impossible to reach, you are responsible for measuring whether you want to do the amount of work required to transform the relationship into one that is likely to meet your needs. And if you try and it doesn't work, it's best for you to take the L and learn from it, not project the failure onto someone who ended up simply *being who they were the whole time.*

You may have often found yourself in emotional loops where you are consistently disappointed by the reality of your relationship(s), while doing incredible amounts of emotional labor, not getting your needs met, and yet somehow remaining endlessly hopeful that things will change. Loop. Loop. Loop. Ad nauseam. It gets exhausting.

The challenge is knowing when to keep hoping, and when to just let go. Even more difficult is taking responsibility for your own role in the pattern you've co-created, and seeing that *you agreed to it* by continuing to participate. It's easy to blame the emotionally damaged or unavailable person, but it is harder and ultimately more useful to see how your own stuff got you here. Often it's your own refusal to see situations objectively, or else a hubris about the magical balm your love and effort can be. (Friendly reminder: you can't "fix" people.)

A gentle acceptance, coupled with the challenge to interrupt these patterns, is the kindest way to treat yourself when you recognize what you're doing and wish to do it differently. So, for example, if you know you're attracted to those "broken bird" types, take an honest inventory as to why that might be. *What does it do for you to pour so much love and energy into someone's cup even once you see their cup has a hole in the bottom and therefore cannot be filled?*

If you know you're attracted to high-drama situations, explore what that might be doing for you. *What kind of negative payoff do you get from walking on eggshells? From not being able to relax? Is there a "family of origin" story there? Is it familiar? Are you afraid what might happen if things were to be calm and peaceful? Does calm always feel to you like "calm before the storm?"*

If you know you're likely to be into people who aren't really that into you, pay attention to what that does for you. *Do you believe yourself to be unworthy of love and so you unconsciously create situations that reinforce this belief? Or perhaps you aren't ready to be in a relationship so you only pursue situations unlikely to work out?*

The thing is: negative payoffs are still highly motivating despite the fact you don't actually enjoy how they feel. You may still get something out of it, much like how someone in active addiction doesn't exactly *enjoy* returning to their source of addiction, because it causes strife in their life, but it does temporarily, in some way, make them feel better.

So take a good look at what you're doing, what your patterns are, and how/ if it aligns with your vision for relationships and what you want things to look like moving forward. Take an inventory and determine in what areas you might be settling. What kinds of things are you doing that make it all harder than it has to be?

I get that sometimes the situations are messy and it's hard to know exactly what to do next. Too, I am sure some of you have been (recently or in the past) cheated on and/or lied to and/or been through the emotional wringer with someone or some situation, independent of a pattern. It makes it hard to even know what it means to "settle" or to identify it when it's happening.

Here are some of my thoughts about all of this that might help you sort out your own thoughts:

First of all, I want to normalize the idea that feeling many things about a person or situation at once is okay. It is okay to feel competing emotions. It is okay to not really know how you feel. It is okay for one day you to feel one way and the next to feel even the exact opposite, or even to feel opposite things at the exact same time. This is called *ambivalence*, and it is normal, as uncomfortable as it may be.

Secondly, it is totally okay to give people another chance if you feel like they deserve it. Even if there are 100 people shouting in your ears not to trust, if you know you need to find something out for sure, sometimes you have to learn something the hard way. I say: go ahead and learn it. Sometimes the only way to lay something to rest is to try it again and have the same result. *(That said, don't go overboard with this; do try and remember that there's something to the adage "fool me once…")*

You could always be surprised. People are so much more than the worst thing they ever did. I believe in grace. I believe in restorative justice and rehabilitation. I believe people are complex and creative, and do things out of desperation that are uncharacteristic of them overall. Decent people do shitty stuff sometimes. So, be open to someone surprising you.

And/but you could likewise be disappointed. This is an inevitable outcome in some cases because sometimes, people don't know how to, or can't, or won't, be better. When you gave them a chance (or many chances) and they didn't show up for you, don't be discouraged. At that point, it's not your problem. That's when you dust yourself off, chalk it up to a lesson learned, and move on.

If you know you're attracted to messy and drama-filled relationships, but this book isn't quite getting to the root, that doesn't mean you don't have root work to do! Please go to therapy. It is worth extra effort to work out whatever of your own stuff makes fixing other people or being mistreated (or whatever is happening) seem more appealing or inevitable than just being in a healthy relationship. Figure out why you might be inclined to "settle" instead of venturing out to look for something better.

Because here is the thing: while there are certainly landmines to navigate, I am nonetheless certain that there *are* decent people out there. There are people who are doing the work it takes to be healthy and emotionally available. I believe there are plenty of people you could meet who won't suck you dry emotionally. I am certain there are people out there who will want what you're offering. I know there are people who want to have a healthy, happy, communicative and easy*ish* relationship *with you*.

If you can't find any, it may be possible that you're not putting off the signals that you're ready for one like that. You too may actually be a broken bird in your own way. And that's all right, you just owe yourself putting in the work to figure it out so you don't find yourself settling for something that isn't serving you.

Never, ever settle.

## Reflection:

*Have you ever knowingly "settled" when you were aware of your own dissatisfaction? What are your insights about why you may have done that? What did it do for you?*

*Would you say your current relationship situation is one where you might be "settling"? What is that about?*

*What reasons might you give for sticking with a situation that you knew wasn't giving you what you needed?*

# LESSON 16: BOUNDARIES

*"Fucked-up people will try to tell you otherwise, but boundaries have nothing to do with whether you love someone or not. They are not judgments, punishments, or betrayals. They are a purely peaceable thing: the basic principles you identify for yourself that define the behaviors that you will tolerate from others, as well as the responses you will have to those behaviors. Boundaries teach people how to treat you, and they teach you how to respect yourself."*
— Cheryl Strayed, Tiny Beautiful Things: Advice on
Love and Life from Dear Sugar

OR

From Wikipedia: *"Personal boundaries are guidelines, rules or limits that a person creates to identify for themselves what are reasonable, safe and permissible ways for other people to behave towards him or her and how they will respond when someone steps past those limits."*

In my experience, some people naturally have stronger boundaries than others. Very empathetic people tend to have a harder time with boundaries, most likely because they feel very invested in other people's well-being. For these folks, merging emotionally with others, or prioritizing the needs of others over their own, often feels like a *good* thing, even an honorable thing. Learning that there is a potentially negative aspect to this altruism, or discovering that maybe "lack of boundaries" is the appropriate phrase to describe their way of being, can be jarring.

People can have a hard time with boundaries for all kinds of reasons. Some people struggle with boundaries because of dysfunctional families of origin. There might be significant emotional distress associated with establishing boundaries due to negative experiences in the past, such that avoiding it altogether simply feels less frightening. Perhaps your relationship with your family is what we call *"enmeshed,"* which basically means members of the family are "inappropriately connected" or "close in a maladaptive or unhealthy way."

Or perhaps your parents taught you that you are to do exactly what you are told without question, even if what was being asked of you wasn't fair or reasonable. Even if what you're told to do violates your own internal value system. This is called "authoritarian parenting" and it's often among the reasons adults have a hard time in relationships as adults, because it's hard to learn how to be assertive and confident if you aren't given space to practice in your formative years. Authoritarian parents teach you to follow orders, but they typically don't teach you how to evaluate whether the orders are worth following. Being raised by this kind of caregiver also lends itself to all kinds of other issues regarding "authority" figures that we won't get into here.

If any of these scenarios was your experience growing up, you may find that you simply never learned to express or prioritize your own thoughts, feelings, and opinions. Maybe you don't even know how to identify them! That's okay. You can start working on this now.

Some people have a difficult time asserting themselves, or feeling entitled to speak up when something doesn't feel good to you. Sometimes this is about low self-esteem, lack of confidence, or a sense of not being worthy. *(We've been talking about these things in various lessons, but you'll start to notice how they creep up all over the place…)*

Some people are "people pleasers" and so you may habitually disregard your own wishes and desires in service of other people. People pleasers are chronically conflict-avoidant and find the idea of upsetting other people intolerable, such that you will choose to suffer rather than risk conflict. People who people-please often try to earn love through being agreeable at all times.

All of these are potentially problematic in the context of relationships, particularly when it comes to establishing and maintaining boundaries. Because regardless of the origin of the difficulty, what often happens is that in failing to hold others' needs, desires, and opinions at an appropriate distance from your own, you may find yourself unable to even accurately determine what you think or feel. You may routinely fail to adequately attend to your own needs, and will begin (or continue) to habitually back-burner yourself. So over time, you may feel exhausted, overwhelmed, and burdened but not even know why, or who to blame for these feelings. You may find saying "No" to be nearly impossible even when you are quite clear you do not want to do the thing you're being asked to do.

So the first step is to begin to tune in to yourself. What do *you* want? How do *you* feel? If you struggle in this area, it is likely you tend to know pretty readily what other people want, need, and feel, so the practice is to begin turning that satellite away from the rest of the world and towards yourself. Use that incredible skill to start really paying attention to your own feelings and deciding what your feelings are asking you to do differently. There's a reason they say on airplanes that we need to put our own oxygen mask on first! You have to be taking care of yourself well in order to have healthy relationships with other people.

So ask yourself: *Where do you need to set boundaries and with whom?* Begin to make a plan. Start small, with a person or people who are pretty easy to negotiate things with or who you know definitely have your best interests in mind. Maybe you have a friend who you always show up for even when you don't really want to. In that case, the practice may be something as minor as saying to them, *"Sometimes when we make plans, I don't feel up to hanging out, but I usually do it anyway because I don't want to upset you. I'm trying to work on being more true to myself, so I just wanted you to know that occasionally I may need to reschedule. Thank you for understanding.*" Your friend may be a bit taken aback, but hopefully they respond well and accept this new boundary. Interestingly, once you feel safe being more honest with them about how you're feeling, you may find yourself *more* interested in actually hanging out because the whole relationship may just feel better.

Not all the boundary-setting will be smooth like this, though. If you've been enmeshed with your mother for 40 years, trying to assert new boundaries with her is probably going to be a challenge. But the practice remains the same. Getting clear first on what you want and how you feel, and prioritizing your own happiness and emotional safety.

It's important to remember that you can only be responsible for setting and maintaining boundaries for yourself, so you have to be prepared to respond if and when others do not honor your stated boundaries. If the people around you do not routinely set or maintain boundaries, you're going to rock the boat by being the first. If you have a long history of *not* having clear or solid boundaries with a specific person, you might even expect that they will become upset or angry when you inform them that they are now expected to behave differently towards you. They might respond with efforts to induce guilty or shameful feelings, or respond by challenging you or pushing back. They may outright reject your boundaries. Prepare yourself for this: generally speaking, *people do not like new boundaries.*

Prior to newly asserting yourself in these challenging relationships, you will want to think carefully about what you're willing to do and how far you're willing to go if this person refuses to honor your stated boundaries. Will you be able to withstand their manipulation or complaints? Will you be able to hang up the phone or block their number or refuse to answer your door? Depending on the person, you may have to deal with some of these extreme behaviors when you begin to instate boundaries. (Don't worry, like the hypothetical case with the friend I mentioned, some people will totally honor your boundaries and it'll be completely okay and smooth. I'm just setting you up to succeed if it happens to be really hard.)

Think of boundaries as being about self-care. It's about putting your oxygen mask on and breathing fully. It is not selfish or self-centered to have boundaries; in fact they are imperative to healthy living. You teach other people how to treat you, what you'll accept, and even what your values are, by how effectively you maintain healthy boundaries. This includes the simple act of learning how to say, "No." ("No" is a complete sentence!)

The reason I caution you about being ready to enforce boundaries before you instate them is that setting boundaries can't work if you're making idle threats. For people who are resistant to your boundaries, if you're wishy-washy about them or you only selectively enforce them, they will be perceived as mixed messages or "crying wolf." Simply put, people won't believe you. You must be prepared to handle resistance, and have a game plan for how to proceed with unwavering consistency. This is all part of getting clear on who you are, what you want, and what kind of relationships you want to have.

## Reflection:

*What comes up for you when you begin to assess your own boundary-setting ability?*

*If you're good at boundary setting, how did you get there? Was it natural or did you have to practice?*

*If you're not yet, are you aware of the origin of the challenges?*

*Where might you start practicing boundary-setting?*

*What do you think might change if you develop greater skill in this area?*

# LESSON 17: INTERDEPENDENCE

In the previous lesson, I talked about "boundaries" mostly in terms of family relationships and friendships, which is super important when we're talking about how to be a healthy, happy person. You have to consistently do that boundary work in all of your relationships. But there's a slightly different framework we can use for intimate relationships. In a partnership, boundaries can be thought of as *"the line at which one person ends and the other person begins."* (Families with poor boundaries are often referred to as "enmeshed," but in intimate relationships we might refer to it as "codependency.")

Predictably, an issue that arises when you are challenged at establishing and maintaining boundaries is that you run the risk of having codependent relationships. People who come from enmeshed families are particularly likely to have codependent relationships in adulthood, for example. These are ones where you over-rely on the opinion and perspective of another person in your decision-making. Or where you and your partner share everything, including all friends and all interests, and maybe even have given up some of your own identity in order to "merge" with your partner. There is a lack of privacy, or even the reasonable expectation of privacy, in a codependent relationship. One obvious sign of this is couples who share a Facebook or email account, for example. It demonstrates a blurred line between you.

So let's talk about healthy boundaries and interdependent relationships, which seem to be the ideal. I like this quote by Harriet Lerner:

*"An intimate relationship is one in which neither party silences, sacrifices, or betrays the self and each party expresses strength and vulnerability, weakness and competence in a balanced way."*

In a healthy relationship, each partner's identity is clearly delineated, but complementary to the other partner's. The relationship dynamic is characterized by "interdependence" as opposed to "codependence" or "independence."

**Interdependence** is the ideal configuration for marriages; it is hallmarked by autonomy and the *ability and willingness* to be separate. It occupies a healthy space where you may *prefer* to be together, but you are *able* to be apart without significant distress. In other words, you really like hanging out with each other, and may mostly choose to do so, but if one of you has other plans, nobody freaks out or takes it personally. You each keep your own friends and have your own interests. Some of your interests may intersect, but when they don't, it's okay to pursue the things you are each interested in. No one begrudges the other their privacy or their space to be an individual. No one feels threatened by an expression of separateness, because emotional connection is maintained even during physical separation. In short, *you feel safe and secure in the relationship even when you can't see your partner.*

Interdependence is characterized by being open to influencing one another, making decisions via collaboration, and each person essentially having your own life in addition to the life you share. You care about each other, but you each maintain your own identity and are responsible for your own emotional state. Like this: *Your feelings may impact me, and they may activate empathy or concern, but I do not become overwhelmed with your feelings such that they become my feelings.*

Now, for some, the incompatible goal of ***independence*** sounds positive or ideal, because you don't want to rely on someone else. Maybe that's just how you are. Or maybe you've been taught by your family or culture that you have to be able to totally make it on your own, and that you don't "need" a partner. Maybe your lived experiences have taught you that you can't trust someone else to have your back. Maybe you let your guard down and were hurt by a partner before and so you refuse to give up your autonomy in any way. I can empathize with all of this fully, and you may or may not be able to undo this conditioning without some help from your therapist.

If the roots are not so deep you can't dig them up yourself, I would invite you to consider this and start digging: being too independent actually makes you hard to partner with. Independence in this context is characterized by a lack of intimacy, refusal to be vulnerable, and rigid boundaries. Independence often means refusing to accept influence from others and being unwilling to compromise. It may look like preferring to keep separate lives entirely, where you're "together but not together." If you're pre-disposed to prefer independence but your partner isn't, you may default to making all your own decisions and fail to check in with your partner, which is certain to cause conflict because they are expecting teamwork.

Again, dig into this. *Where can you make some shifts? What healing or mind-changing would have to take place in order for you to slide a little down the continuum from "independence" to at least a willingness for "interdependence?" What conversations do you need to have with your partner in order for this to be easier?*

I like this quote, too:

*"Let there be spaces in your togetherness, And let the winds of the heavens dance between you. Love one another but make not a bond of love: Let it rather be a moving sea between the shores of your souls. Fill each other's cup but drink not from one cup. Give one another of your bread but eat not from the same loaf. Sing and dance together and be joyous, but let each one of you be alone, Even as the strings of a lute are alone though they quiver with the same music. Give your hearts, but not into each other's keeping. For only the hand of Life can contain your hearts. And stand together, yet not too near together: For the pillars of the temple stand apart, And the oak tree and the cypress grow not in each other's shadow."*

— Kahlil Gibran, "The Prophet"

This quote speaks to the idea of codependence as unhealthy, and inter-dependence as ideal, which is my perspective as well. I tell my clients regularly that the only way to have a truly healthy relationship is to make sure you are intact, that you are a whole person on your own. Do whatever work is involved to ensure you're someone who understands yourself and can express your needs and desires directly. Whatever those may be, I am certain you're always better off making it clear from the very beginning. The right person is going to be totally fine with your unique idiosyncratic ways, and be willing to allow space in your togetherness if that is what you need and ask for.

Too, make sure you are healthy (or working on it…maybe at least healthy*ish)* so that you can recognize and attract healthy people. And then invite your main person to be the cherry on top of an already complete sundae; it is not sustainable to require that they be your whole sundae. *(That's codepen-dence, in a nutshell.)* You have to be and maintain separate sundaes. Healthy relationships contain no ownership or possession, merely the continual agreement of being together by active choice.

## Reflection:

*Out of interdependence, codependence, and independence, which feels most natural to you?*

*Are you clear on the origin of your challenges?*

*Are your challenges around boundaries more prevalent in intimate partnerships or other relationships?*

# LESSON 18: WHAT GETS IN YOUR WAY?

*"You must love in such a way that the person you love feels free."*
—Thich Nhat Hanh

I'm very fond of the idea that every relationship has its own culture, and that idea has become part of my "brand" as a couples' counselor. What I mean by this is: if the dynamics of a relationship are working for the people in it, and everyone would sincerely self-report that they are happy, then regardless of what the world may think of how they're doing it, it's technically "healthy."

Of course, health and functionality are somewhat relative, but in my experience the general thematic element is that in happy relationships, *people feel free.* Free to be entirely themselves, free to communicate fully, free to be vulnerable. When you feel free, you breathe easier, and you are better able to navigate the conflicts and problems that life presents, which it will. (I am writing this in the midst of a global pandemic, for crying out loud. *Life will present problems!*)

My main objective in writing this book is to aggressively and enthusiastically dispel the myth that relationships which are "worth it" are necessarily going to be hard. A relationship that is relatively easy isn't less "real" than one you struggle in. Most importantly, it's simply not true that hard work *in and of itself* is valuable. Many successful endeavors require hard work and dedication, of course, but that doesn't mean that things aren't worth doing if they come somewhat easily to us. We seem to live in a culture that rewards struggle and weirdly resents it when someone seems to naturally excel at something, but that doesn't make sense. Suffering and difficulty should not be ideals to strive for; it seems logical to me that we should strive for happiness and a sense of relative ease.

It's parenthetical in the title, but for clarification I want to stress the word "relative" for a moment and explain what I mean. Relativity is key to evaluating whether a relationship is actually "easy" or not, because what's easy for me may be challenging for you, and vice versa, so there's no generic formula I can apply that will result in "ease." Instead, my working theory about relationships is that it is reasonable to expect that if you're a good fit, more often than not, it should feel pretty easy to be with and connect with someone you're in a significant relationship with.

Specifically, I mean this in an *"Easy like Sunday morning"* kind of way. (Insert Lionel Richie meme here.) In an *"I can easily understand what you're trying to say to me"* kind of way. In an *"It is easy for me to remember why I love you"* kind of way. In a *"You easily make me feel seen and valued in a way that I can equally easily receive"* kind of way. I refer to this as being "relatively easy" or "easy*ish*" and I'll be using the term "relative ease" quite a bit in the coming lessons.

Fun fact: I was originally going to name this book "Easy" and frame it entirely around the idea that you should be able to expect relative ease in a healthy relationship. The premise has since expanded to include the importance of loving yourself and a multitude of other ideas, but I still hold fast to this main thesis. Even the relationship with yourself should ultimately feel "easy*ish*," even in the midst of intense healing work. Not without effort, and not expecting perfection, but mostly pretty smooth and easy because you're in alignment with your truest nature.

I really hope you pay attention and take this idea to heart. The thing is:

what comes more naturally feels better, is more enjoyable, and allows you to more readily engage with the pleasure and satisfaction of *doing the thing well*. This is not to say that you don't have to work hard at things you have some natural ability around, just that it doesn't make sense to intrinsically regard success via hard work as being more valuable than success without struggle.

We have received a strange and counterintuitive cultural lesson that in order to have a healthy, happy relationship, you must invest a great deal of blood, sweat, and tears. We've romanticized the idea that someone ought to "fight" for love, or sacrifice everything, or suffer for it. People often value this brute force of "making" it work instead of what makes more sense to me, which is investing what a relationship really needs -*time and grace and the skills to navigate it*- and expecting it to grow in a natural, healthy way. Being willing to nourish it along, of course, but with the expectation that when planted in good soil, it will be largely self-sustaining.

I have a tattoo on my leg that is a line from a Marge Piercy poem called "The Implications of One Plus One" that reads: *"Timing, chemistry, magic and will and luck."* At the end of the day, I really think that is what a healthy, sustainable, easy*ish* relationship needs. I think *that* is the recipe (+ freedom). Please note that nowhere in the recipe do I list pain, suffering, or arduous effort.

This hard work, "lie in the bed that you've made" messaging about relationships and marriage seems to have myriad roots that intersect, including archaic heteronormative standards rooted in patriarchy and Judeo-Christian values. On the surface, the idea of sacrificing all others for your "one and only" seems lofty and ideal. But the reality of it often leaves people feeling stuck, unhappy, and inadequate in relationships, even though you are expected to keep working hard at them. Because hard work is the reward, I guess, but I think it's really more because you are expected to lie in the beds you've made. The added religious pressure of having committed "till death do us part" before God keeps people trapped in miserable marriages, "working hard" for some reward to be granted later, ostensibly in heaven. This doesn't resonate with me, personally, and I'd invite you to critically consider whether it does with you.

Unfortunately, even today, we are socialized by this culture to believe that our "job" (especially as women) is to find a partner, marry them, have children, and stay together forever, no matter what. It is hard to avoid the pressure of this default life path. One of the major obstacles for finding the easy*ish* relationships you desire is that you are trained to believe they do not exist. You receive messaging that it is not fair or reasonable to want, much less expect, to feel free and easy within your primary intimate relationships.

And when you do get married, you vow it in front of a judge or god(s) and everyone, and then you file a contract with the state that you know will be expensive to break, thereby providing another incentive to keep working.

You are told it is reasonable to expect that this one person will magically be able to meet your needs at every stage of your life, and that they will successfully evolve and change with you as you grow and change. Which you will, because people do, but the reality is there is no guarantee that you will communicate your changes clearly or that your partner will be able or willing to change and evolve with you. If you aren't both skilled at communicating what these needs are as they change and evolve, or if you consistently avoid addressing whatever the issues are because you are afraid it will cause pain, heartache, or conflict, you will find yourself resentful that your "one person" doesn't or can't give you what you need.

But, first of all, as I'll discuss more in later lessons, no one can possibly give you everything. Full stop. But more importantly, *you can't be mad when you don't get things you didn't ask for.* In other words: people are not mind-readers nor miracle workers. Also, it is unreasonable to expect that brute hard work, in the vein of hammering away at a problem that really requires some more delicate tools (tools which you don't happen to have in your toolbox) is going to sufficiently create a happy life.

Like, it's great to have a date night once a week or whatever, but if you actually don't really like each other or have anything substantial to talk about, that date night in and of itself isn't going to do anything to heal the actual problems. You'll just be highlighting them via uncomfortable hours spent together each week. The "good will" account of the relationship has to be consistently kept pretty full in order for this date night to add any meaningful value. The date night can't be the extent of the investment. If you aren't routinely depositing into the account, you can expect that any minor issue or conflict could potentially overdraft it, so you have to be intentional about making sure you stay in the black. "Date night" alone isn't going to cut it.

Another thing that potentially gets in the way: we are inundated with messaging about the scarcity of "good men" or "good women" out there. It's like, if you land a "good one" *(on paper, whatever that looks like or means for you)* you should hang on forever -at all costs- because society suggests that you may never find another one. Let me give you the short answer as to why this idea is bullshit: there are literally billions of people in the world. The idea that you found the only one who has $X$ *desirable qualities* (despite $Y$ *other qualities* that do not work for you or are even harmful to you) is absurd and logically unsound.

Think about a relationship you've had that felt really, really challenging and which ultimately failed. Depending on your stage of life, you may have more or fewer of these. I'm in my 40s, and so I could raise my hand like eight times, but some of you may not have had as much opportunity as I have for messing up relationships. But assuming you have at least one of these in your past, I want you to picture that relationship in your mind. Think about how it felt, and why you ultimately didn't stay together. What do you think you would have needed in order to "make it work?" Perseverance? Patience? Commitment?

I'm going to go out on a limb and suggest the simplest explanation, by which I mean the main problem could probably be summed up as a *lack of basic skills*. It's not a perfect science, and adding or subtracting specific qualities or attributes may have extended the relationship's lifespan, but my guess is (if you were otherwise a good fit) you both mostly needed better skills. Both of you have to at least *be able* to do relationships well. Because while the relationship may still not have worked out due to myriad other factors, including temperamental compatibility, with increased skill it would almost certainly have been far less messy, challenging, and frustrating along the way.

The thing is: nobody is born with relationship skills. Nobody teaches us How To Do Relationships. A huge part of why relationships are so challenging for so many people isn't that we are all mismatched or broken; it's more that we don't actually *learn how to have them*. It's not included in any of our routine educational endeavors. We don't get to take high school or college courses called *Intimate Communication 101* or *How To Date Well* or *Let's Unpack That Issue Before It Destroys Your Marriage*. At some point in our youth, we just start running into each other and fumbling around and trying to make Good Things happen.

Spoiler Alert: mostly, the things that happen are not that good. Mostly, we make a mess.

The good news? It's normal. Everybody goes through this steep learning curve, and while of course there are exceptions, it seems fair to say that most people move into adulthood significantly lacking skills in this area. Most people would report that they believe relationships are "hard work." It is commonly believed that sustaining healthy communication and doing conflict well is "challenging." If this is your opinion or understanding about relationships, you're in good company because most people agree with you.

However, I decidedly do not agree.

I am here to tell you that it doesn't have to be so hard. In fact, I think it is reasonable to expect that more often than not there should be the aforementioned sense of "relative ease" to the connection and that the greater your skill, the easier things become. It still won't be perfect. It will still be more aptly described as "easy*ish*" but surely that's a whole lot better than expecting a lifetime of hard work. As you develop skills and broaden your expectations of what relationships can be and feel like, the better you also get at recognizing when your efforts are not sound investments.

I have observed that a lot of you waste a great deal of time and energy in relationships that do not provide you with this sense of ease, and which actually more often add stress and undue frustration to your lives. Most of you can acknowledge that you have spent months or years of your lives floundering in unsatisfying relationships, confused about what to do.

*Let's just face it: Most people are really bad at relationships, but it's not your fault.*

The funny thing is that many people are bad at relationships in the same predictable ways, which include: *difficulty communicating, fear of vulnerability, lots of shame around sex,* and *fear of conflict.* I guess that's why people are somewhat resistant to my main thesis for this book, which can be neatly summed up thusly: *Relationships should be relatively easy.* People seem almost hurt by this idea, because it flies in the face of so much of what we think we know. It defies the basic understanding many of us are working with when it comes to framing our relationships and their fundamental value.

If you develop skills in the Relationship Department, you will naturally find relating to be easier and less laborious. You will also feel less alarmed when you realize that maybe *this* relationship isn't the right one, because you'll have the confidence to try again. You will know that you *can* do it, and it doesn't have to be that hard, aka "easy*ish,*" when you're in the right situation.

Now, I don't mean you will never have to put in effort, or that things can always be smooth and conflict-free, or that there aren't going to be speed-bumps, detours, and challenges in any significant relationship. It would be unrealistic to suggest that. Humans are complicated and messy, and relationships necessarily grow and change over time, which can be difficult to navigate on occasion.

Key words: *on occasion.*

But let me be clear: in general, it should feel pretty easy to be with and connect with someone with whom you're in a significant relationship. So I would invite you to consider the value in languishing in a relationship that feels like a lot of hard work all the time. It seems unlikely to provide long-term, sustainable happiness, and yet many of us do it anyway. This is what gets in our way, collectively.

Relationships rooted in ease of connection will naturally allow for each of you to grow and change, which of course you will. My advice for starting this reframing process is to pay attention to when and with whom you feel easily connected as well as where you feel free, and to prioritize those feelings. Don't let preconceived notions about what relationships are "supposed" to be get in your way.

And as we move into Part Two, remember that you don't have to use any or all of this, specifically. These are merely suggestions and offerings to put you on a path towards an "easy*ish*" relationship with yourself, whatever that looks like for you.

That way, if you go into a relationship knowing yourself well, and being willing and excited to present that self authentically to someone else, you're positioning yourself to have better success and a much easier time. So doing *some iteration* of this internal work is paramount if your goal is a healthy, vulnerable, mutually beneficial relationship that is relatively easy, but there's no wrong way to do that. Spend as much time here as you need, gathering together your ideas and feelings about who you are and what you want in a relationship. Do your therapy, see your alternative healers, create your vision boards. Whatever you need to get you ready.

Then, I think the key is to hold your vision in mind, and/but be flexible when presented with the ideas and feelings of potential partners. They may have even better ideas from their work on themselves, or from what they've learned from their own history of mistakes, and you may find that you learn from them. You may shift significantly. All of that is great, when sourced from an authentic place within each of you. Just commit to the growth and don't let lack of skills continue to get in your way!

## Reflection:

*What messaging have you gotten about relationships and hard work as it relates to commitment?*

*Have you ever critically examined that messaging and determined what you personally believe and don't believe?*

*What gets in the way for you, specifically?*

*Have many or most of your relationships required a great deal of effort? If so, was the work worth it?*

*Would you (or have you) stayed in a relationship that has stagnated just because you are legally "married" and therefore feel obligated/stuck, even if you wanted to leave?*

# PART TWO:

# RELATIONSHIP WITH
# SOMEONE ELSE

# LESSON 1: WHAT IS A HEALTHY RELATIONSHIP?

**M**any of us don't even really know what it means to have a healthy relationship. There doesn't seem to be a universal definition, and so we will work with mine until you craft your own.

Here it is: I believe that relationship health is relative, and that if it's working for you both, and you would self-report feeling mostly happy, then the relationship is "normal" and can be considered "healthy." I'll keep giving you different perspectives and things to look for and options to consider, but for the sake of this lesson, I offer you the shortest version possible of how to assess it: a healthy relationship will be hallmarked by what I refer to as *"relative ease."* What does this mean? Here are some things to look for:

It does not feel like a ton of work all of the time.

It does not feel like pulling teeth to effectively communicate.

You do not have to fight to be heard.

A basic respect and kindness consistently resonates between you and your partner, even under stress. You treat each other with unconditional positive regard.

There will probably be rough patches, but the overarching nature of the relationship is such that it is your soft place to land at the end of a hard day. It is not the hard part.

In short, relationships should not be super challenging all the time, and people should not give up their entire lives trying to make it work if it is just *not working*. Additionally, it is crucial that you know that there are any number of reasons relationships don't work, many of which are no one's fault. Some are even relatively predictable insofar as I see the same outcomes over and over.

For example, some people are *fundamentally and at their core* not a good fit. Temperament, used here to describe the parts of people's personalities that are pretty fixed and organic, informs who we are and how we behave. While of course you can theoretically "make it work" with anyone, some temperaments are not compatible, if by "compatible" we mean *"can find relative ease in being together."* Some personalities just rub each other the wrong way and so you are always likely to feel like there's inherent friction or tension when you simply try to exist together. (I'll discuss more in the lesson about compatibility and dealbreakers.)

Some people cannot, or if I'm being less generous, *will not*, heal from past wounds or forgive past transgressions. There are some issues that relationships never move on from, and I would implore you not to agree to live in purgatory if it seems clear you've landed at one of these impasses. Give it a fair amount of time, and try whatever is at your disposal to move through it, but then if your person seems clear that they cannot "get over" whatever the thing is, even with conscientious effort, it might be best to move on. Sometimes it's worth the pain of moving on just to have access to a clean slate again.

If you cannot forgive regularly, often, and generously, then you will probably not be happy together. I write more about forgiveness in a later lesson, but the gist is that healthy relationships *(those that are hallmarked with relative ease and overarching kindness)* require a pretty continual flow of radical grace and radical forgiveness. Radical grace is the willingness to offer the benefit of the doubt at all times. It is the willingness and ability to offer reflexive forgiveness, as opposed to score-keeping or punishment, of the daily transgressions that are inevitable in a long-term committed relationship.

Yes, I said *daily* and *inevitable.* Because even with the best of intentions, people are going to mess up, annoy, frustrate, say the wrong thing, and even cause hurt and pain. It's the built-in risk of engaging in long-term relationships with other humans. But when both of you are quick to offer grace, apologize and move on, it can be relatively painless to navigate the relationship, namely because you're freed from having to worry that every minor issue may escalate to a bigger one.

Another reason a relationship might not work is that some people are simply not emotionally well enough at this particular stage in their life to be able to maintain a healthy relationship. Often, this is a result of events in their life beyond their control, like unresolved trauma history, challenging mental health diagnoses, or the lingering effects of previous unhealthy or abusive relationships. Sometimes their families of origin were deeply dysfunctional in a way that makes it difficult for them as adults to trust, to connect, and to be affectionate or intimate.

It is important that anyone who identifies with these struggles know: you are not a lost cause. You are not just "destined to be alone." People in situations like these need, want, desire, and deserve healthy relationships. You deserve to feel emotionally safe and connected. Full stop. *And also* you will probably need to be working on your own stuff before you can be all the way invested in a meaningful intimate relationship *in a healthy way with healthy boundaries*.

Yes, even those with significant mental health diagnoses can have relatively "easy" relationships, with mindfulness and consistent attention paid to managing your own stuff. Finding a good therapist, establishing healthy habits, and adhering to medication schedules can all work wonders in helping get you to a place where you are happy and healthy and open to connecting intimately. Let me say it again because I want to be very clear: being challenged in this (or any) area is not synonymous to being somehow undeserving. We are all deserving of solid, healthy, supportive, grace-full relationships.

My initial advice is simple, however, before we dive in further: don't waste your time languishing or gathering evidence if you already know in your bones that you aren't right for each other or you simply can't find a way to be happy together. Life is short, and promises nothing.

So it is not a failure to say, *"I've had enough"* if the relationship you're in isn't making you happy. It is not greedy to insist that your relationship be rich, supportive, loving, and open. It is not too much to want to be your whole, fully-authentic self in a relationship and not have someone insist that you fundamentally change who you are.

It is not selfish to say, *"I want to be happy."*

A good, healthy relationship is one in which you are whole, and your partner is whole, and you regularly choose to be together out of desire rather than need or habit. I always tell people this: don't try to fill a space with someone else. It doesn't work. You have to learn to fill it yourself, and *then* invite someone in. Even if you're still learning, and practicing, and occasionally falling short. That's okay.

In my work, I have seen hundreds of couples attempt to navigate life together under varying circumstances, and I think it's imperative to understand that A Serious Relationship is essentially a DIY *(do-it-yourself)* project. You are building and co-creating a space where there wasn't one before, and there are no rules or directions. You can, and should, get creative. In fact, the more creativity and authenticity you bring, the greater the likelihood is that you will feel satisfied by what you've built. Because when we frame relationships in this way, it is clear that whatever you co-create is both of your fault, if there is fault to be distributed, and both of your responsibility, as well.

Okay, so as we move into more lessons on being in relationship with other people, let me introduce my main guiding principles as a couples' counselor. They are as follows:

- There is no such thing as "normal" or "typical" when it comes to how to do relationships.

- The more you try to live up to some ideal standard, the more disappointed you're likely to feel. Nobody's relationship is perfect, despite what social media might have you believe. *Perfection is not a thing.*

- Every single relationship has its own culture. By this I mean it will have its own unique rules, norms, and standards of behavior. You create these together, whether intentionally or unintentionally.

- It is decidedly better to do it intentionally.

- Every relationship should be open to re-negotiation of the agreements you've made with each other. At any point, you should be able to say, *"I no longer agree to this. We need to renegotiate,"* and be heard by your partner (or partners, if you're non-monogamous).

- If everyone is having their needs met, and you're being honest and open with each other, whatever you decide to do or not do in the context of the relationship is okay and "normal" for you.

- A healthy relationship is one in which you are encouraged to be your most authentic self, where it is safe to express your vulnerabilities, and where you feel supported and appreciated. A healthy relationship is, by definition, *relatively easy.* Easy*ish.*

Note: I want to add here that throughout this book, there will always be exceptions for abusive relationships. Relationships in which abuse is present are not just "challenging" and you shouldn't be expected to "take responsibility for co-creating the problems," etc. If you are being asked to take responsibility for your own abuse, that is abuse in itself.

Your abuser is probably gaslighting you, which means, basically, making you feel crazy. They may try to convince you that the things they do are your fault. Please note that if that is your story, these rules do not apply to you. You did not DIY yourself into a situation where you are being harmed, belittled, or coerced. You deserve to be safe and happy, and a person who is hurting you is not a good partner for you. I hope you can find the courage and the resources to leave, but if you cannot, please know I am not judging you for being or staying where you are. There are many resources for victims of emotional and physical violence; please get help if you need it and do NOT blame yourself.

## Reflection:

*Which of my guiding principles do you agree with, and which do you disagree with?*

*Do you agree that every relationship has its own culture and makes its own rules?*

*What are your thoughts about what makes a healthy relationship?*

*Based on that criteria, have most of your relationships been healthy? Spend a little time reflecting here.*

# LESSON 2: EVERY RELATIONSHIP HAS ITS OWN CULTURE

*"To be yourself in a world that is constantly trying to make you something else is the greatest accomplishment."* —Ralph Waldo Emerson

L et me expand a bit, because this is one of the main takeaways I hope you'll receive from this book. I believe that while there are guidelines and considerations for measuring the overall health of a relationship *(including some things that are objectively harmful, like violence, for example)*, it is also true that there is actually no such thing as a "normal relationship." You and whoever you're in relationship with are a unique combination that has never before been seen.

*"Every relationship has its own culture"* is a thing I say a lot. Of course, there are plenty of rules and conventions that people do hold themselves to, a lot of "shoulds" and "ought tos" when it comes to what people seem to think a relationship should look like. But in actual practice, there is no such thing as a "typical" relationship, so trying to live up to some nebulous standard is a recipe for disappointment.

You can literally quote me on this, *"If you're both having your needs met, and you're being honest and open with each other then generally speaking, whatever you decide to do or not do in the context of the relationship is okay and 'normal' for you."* (Amy L. Miller, LCSW, 2020).

Here's an example from my own life: my husband and I don't sleep in the same bed, and it is awesome. I cannot overstate this fact: I am actively grateful every single day and night to have my own space. (I now have my own bathroom, as well!) Honestly, I think it's a major reason we have cohabitated peacefully these past five years. I am so thankful he's comfortable with this arrangement because I have lived with two other partners in the past, and in both cases I wasn't even given the option to not share a bed.

Wait. I should say that a different way, because the truth is, we actually never discussed it. So if I am being fair, I have to admit that I co-created the situation *(that is, bed-sharing that I didn't want to do)* by not asking for it to be different. I do remember looking forward to sleeping alone on the rare occasion I was out of town or my (now ex) husband was working overnight and I got a bed to myself by default. But I never *asked* to be able to consistently sleep alone, so I can't fairly blame the other person for not giving me what I wanted.

I think if I had known at the time that it was okay to advocate for my own needs, I would have insisted on my own bed *even if it caused conflict in the relationship,* which it very well may have. In both of these cases, I did make sure I had my own room in the house for my computer and music collection, which sort of met this need, but I actually think that it's having my own bed that is really important to me and makes me happy. But like most of us, I have been indoctrinated with ideas about what relationships are "supposed" to look like and what you "should" do when you're involved with someone.

It honestly didn't occur to me until this most recent relationship that doing things differently in this way was even an option. I thought if you're in a serious relationship and live together, it must signal a problem if you don't sleep in the same bed. I no longer believe this, because I now, much more deeply than ever before, believe instead: *"If it's working for both of you and you would self-report that you're happy, whatever you're doing or not doing is okay and healthy."*

I don't necessarily advertise to the world that we don't sleep together, but it's not a secret. Especially since I am absolutely certain it means nothing about the health of the relationship and it doesn't signal pending disaster. We've lived together, quite happily, for years now. I use it as an example for clients all the time when they're trying to navigate sleep issues, or just as a simple example of doing things differently than "the norm" and how that can be perfectly fine.

What we have found is that it works better for us to be well-rested and happy in separate sleeping spaces than to force ourselves to live by a convention that isn't even that important to either of us. We have discussed the fact that if at any point sleeping together feels like an important thing to try, for either of us, we can revisit it. This is crucial because it includes an option for things to change or for feelings to evolve, which is normal and healthy over the course of a relationship's lifespan.

So it is not actually a problem that we are incompatible sleeping partners, or that I generally prefer to sleep alone, because that has an easy fix: just don't sleep together. But it *would* be a problem if we ignored our incompatibilities and insisted on sleeping in the same bed anyway because that is *just what you do.* I would be so annoyed and angry over something that he literally cannot help: snoring. Also, we like to go to bed at different times, so he'd be waking me up every night when he came to bed. I prefer a rock hard mattress; I like it freezing cold and pile on tons of blankets. I also use a weighted blanket. He likes a soft squishy mattress and for it to be warm enough not to need a pile of blankets. These things simply don't go well together and it would almost certainly cause unnecessary conflict.

If we were to force it, I'm afraid we might not even still be living together! That would be a shame, right? There is nothing fundamentally wrong with the relationship, but if we chose to force this particular thing, it could conceivably trickle into other aspects of the relationship.

Seems pretty straightforward, right? But for whatever reason, many couples do not ever pause to consider whether, to use this example, sleeping together is actually something that is important to them, or whether they might actually prefer to sleep separately. They might not know or believe that either way is *totally healthy and okay.* You can still maintain a robust sex life and a deep emotional connection, and get enough quality time without sleeping in the same bed. You just may have to be more intentional about some of those things, but your relationship will also benefit from the added attention.

There are many other conventions I see couples habitually adhere to. Some couples do not stop to reconsider *any* of the myriad conventions that we think of as the "default settings" of relationships. So I am here to suggest, perhaps radically, that basically *everything* is open to negotiation, and there are no rules or limits. As I said before, it is essentially a DIY project: *You are building and co-creating a brand new space where there wasn't one before and there are no rules or directions. You can, and should, get creative. Every relationship has its own culture.*

## Reflection:

*If you're currently partnered, what conventions are you living by in your relationship that you haven't fully considered?*

*Is your vision of an ideal relationship one that's never been done before? What would it take for you to create the vision you hold?*

*If you could change one thing about your current relationship, what would it be? Imagine talking to your partner about that one thing; how might it go?*

# LESSON 3: DEAL BREAKERS AND COMPATIBILITY

This is a potentially controversial topic, but I think human temperament is *congenital,* meaning it is with you from birth. Anyone who has children can attest to the fact that, to some extent, your child is born *who they are.* You can raise them with certain values, teach them the things that are important to you, and even punish them for displaying behaviors that you don't like. Over time, they may adapt to the expectations of their family and the broader society. But that doesn't change their core nature, which is relatively fixed.

So remember when I said that some people are *fundamentally and at their core* not a good fit together? Accepting my core tenet about temperament is necessary in order for you to go with me on this next lesson. Temperament informs not only how we behave, but to some extent, it defines who we are. While you can probably "make it work" with anyone, some temperaments are simply not compatible, if by "compatible" we mean *"can find relative ease in being together."* Some temperaments are likely to consistently feel like there's inherent friction or tension in just existing together.

The real question here then is: *if just being who you are is annoying or frustrating to someone else, why would you want to spend your life proving to them that you're okay how you are or trying to morph into what they think you should be?*

Because of how we're socialized, this whole *"working really hard against our fundamental natures for the good of this relationship"* thing may seem like the kind of hard work that's worth it, but if you never find yourself able to relax into the connection or rely on it to be a source of comfort, I want to suggest gently that you might be better off taking care of yourself for a while. Then, when you're ready, get back out there to find someone you're a better fit with. *(Always keep in mind that there are literally billions of people in the world!)*

Here's the thing: if you enter the relationship with the idea in mind that this person will either willingly change (unlikely) or that you will be able to *make them* change (even less likely) you are setting yourself up for failure. You have to sincerely like the person, in their current form, from the get-go, and accept that they are basically who they are going to be, in order to enter honestly and joyfully into a sustainable relationship together.

It is my firm opinion that people do not change. To be clear, behaviors can change, attitudes can change, desires change, and *capacity for changing* changes, but *who you are at your most authentic and core self* does not.

To that end, I don't accept everything about the Myers-Briggs Type Indicator (MBTI®) system, but I do believe the core tenet that Jung presents, which is that temperament is inborn or "nature," and as such I do not believe it is wise to willingly enter into relationships that require you to routinely work against your nature. This is why I find the MBTI® useful in couples' work; once I know each person's best-fit type, it helps me efficiently and quickly pinpoint what some of the issues are likely to be.

We will work on learning to spot those incompatibilities, and recognizing when those challenging relationships are not the relationships where your effort is best spent. My goal is to offer you plenty of practical tips and tools designed to immediately enhance your skill and increase the probability of partnering well.

First and foremost, please remember that there is no such thing as the "perfect" person for you. There are infinite possibilities of relationships you could have, many of which would result in similar levels of self-reported happiness, and all of which rely on the happenstance that you cross paths with certain compatible people. At any given time, you are merely playing the odds and trying to pick the best one based on the people you come across and the timing of those encounters.

I want to acknowledge that it is truly a crapshoot and doesn't seem to be particularly fair, so if you are not experiencing what you would call "luck" in this area, I don't want you to just assume it is your fault. Lots of amazing and wonderful people desperately want relationships, and would be good at them, and can't seem to find them, while others seem to be able to have anyone they want and don't even seem to appreciate the gift that is.

It can often feel like there's no justice in this search for connection. Unfortunately, I don't have a magic solution. I wish I did! Ultimately, I think all you can really do is remain open to the idea that, based on statistics alone, there are *definitely* people out there who want what you want. There are definitely people who will happily accept and reciprocate what you are offering. In whatever ways feel good to you, I would suggest you keep trying to put yourself in their path or be where people you could potentially connect with are. This could mean anything from dating apps to meet-up groups to letting friends set you up on blind dates to just being friendly and open, in general.

I used to also say there was no such thing as soulmates, but I don't know if I believe that anymore. I've gotten a bit more, as they say, "woo woo" in my old age. I think my current belief can be more accurately explained thusly: we could have many soulmates throughout our lives who come and go for various reasons. I think I've encountered a fair number of my "soul mates" in my life, and I believe my current husband is one. I don't necessarily think we magically end up with someone because they are "predestined" for us, though. I don't think that makes sense; it's too limiting and too dependent upon chance encounters. *(I mean, as I said before: there are literally billions of people in the world.)*

But all that being said, I definitely think you have to deeply consider what you want, need, and "have to have" in your relationships well before you find yourself faced with real decisions regarding such things. There are some dynamics, qualities, or situations that you may know you will never be able to work with. I had you list some of these things in the first part of the book. Get that list out or make it now if you skipped it before, because this is relevant.

Questions like this: *when you think about your "dealbreakers" or the things you simply must have, or conversely, cannot abide in a relationship, what are they? Have they changed over time? If you're currently happily partnered, are there aspects of your partner or this relationship that at other points in your life you couldn't have imagined would work for you?*

It is useful to have some general ideas about what is most important to you in your intimate relationships, but I also know that things look and feel different coming from different people. What I mean is, it's easy to get very black and white about things in the abstract, but they may become more grey when they are part of an actual human interaction.

Here is an example: suppose you are a longtime vegetarian and you believe you could never be with someone who ate meat. It violates your core values and you *simply cannot imagine*. Then you happen to meet someone who is everything you want in a person. They are funny, kind, smart, successful, attractive…but you quickly learn that they are also an unapologetic omnivore and completely unwilling to consider becoming vegetarian, even for wonderful you.

In this case, you will have to make some decisions, right? Namely, are you willing to throw away the potential you see in this relationship in order to honor a deeply-held value like this? Or are you more likely to amend your dealbreakers list from *"must be vegetarian"* to perhaps, *"must understand and support why being vegetarian is important to me?"*

Another example is this extremely salient question about whether we can effectively and happily partner with people whose political beliefs are different than (or even opposed to) our own. In the current climate of deep political divisiveness, I personally find it difficult to imagine having an easy relationship from "across the aisle," as it were. But I also recognize that, for me, my political beliefs are intrinsically tied to my values, so someone who doesn't agree with me politically is likely to also have fundamentally different values. There are some areas I might be able to compromise, whereas in other areas I definitely cannot. That said, I know that other people feel less connected to their political beliefs, in which case having differing views on issues might not be a dealbreaker.

It is important to note that there's really not right or wrong answers here, because only you can weigh your opinions and values and predict how likely certain things are to truly bother you over time. The useful practice is taking the time to consider, perhaps for the first time, which things you *may* actually be more flexible on when it comes down to it, as opposed to which are decidedly firm.

As well, it's relevant to note that many behaviors or qualities we think are extremely important in theory, either "must have" or "must not have," may not end up being dealbreakers when a specific person has them. For example, I might have said at some point that it was very important to me that someone be an "on-time" person in order for me to partner well with them and be happy. Being punctual is important to me, and I despise being late.

My husband is decidedly *not* an "on-time" person. But instead of tossing him aside for not meeting my requirement, I've instead had to modify my approach to how we get places on time. Now, I'm not saying this is the best or most ethical way to deal with this, but the truth is sometimes I lie to him *just a little bit* about what time we have to be places, especially doctor's appointments and the like. I tell him it's like ten minutes earlier than it really is. It works out because then I am free to not stress, to not be cranky or agitated, and to not be annoyed with him...and we end up actually getting there early or on actual time. Win/win, right?!

I say this to say that I necessarily downgraded my initial "must have" to a simple "would be nice" upon getting to know *this particular person*, which has by now simply landed at "doesn't really matter." I was willing to reflexively do this in order to make room for who he specifically is, in part because I have realized that the positive side of this annoying "perpetually late/lack of urgency" quality he has is a certain relaxed, patient, low-anxiety quality that I actually really appreciate. But I couldn't know that from the get-go, so had I insisted on sticking to my timeliness requirement, I'd have missed out on the love of my life and the peace he regularly brings to my life with his (also annoying) lackadaisical temperament. Make sense?

So when you think about what you have to have or what you cannot tolerate, I'd invite you to be a little bit curious and flexible where you can. Ask yourself:

*Are there qualities, characteristics, beliefs, or behaviors that you absolutely know you cannot tolerate? What are those things? Can you imagine situations where you might be willing to be flexible on even those, if many other things you really want or need are clearly present?*

It is also extremely useful to consider what the inverse may be of the qualities you do or don't want in a person. As I said about my husband, the quality that is potentially annoying about him (lack of urgency) has a corresponding positive quality (patience) woven in. If I magically changed his urgency, maybe ramped it up a little, he might go from a guy who's incredibly patient and accepting of me (which I appreciate) to a guy who's always rushing me and getting impatient (which would stress me out). In the end, I see how I can't have the thing I like without accepting the thing that's frustrating. That helps me to reframe my annoyance and find ways to live with it, and even appreciate it. So ultimately, while it's still sometimes frustrating when he doesn't move quickly, I would not change anything about him even if I could, because the positive aspects far outweigh any annoyances.

I often advise clients in couples' work to consider this question broadly when they're in a state of perpetual annoyance with each other. I ask them to think about what desirable qualities they might be giving up about their partner if they traded in the attribute they dislike or find annoying. If you try this exercise, even with other people in your life besides an intimate partner, you may find it eye-opening to consider how connected these qualities are. Spend a little time on these ideas and see what you think about your own strengths, weaknesses, and potentially annoying qualities! Does this change anything about the way you frame other people's?

As is often the case when pondering how to do relationships, there are no right or wrong answers. I just want you to start thinking critically about how compatibility actually works. Another way to think of it is 80/20. It seems reasonable to suppose that someone can -at best- check maybe 80% of your boxes.

It is up to you to determine the relative weight of each criterion so that you can determine what adds up to 80% *for you*. Depending on your life circumstances thus far, those crucial factors may look very different for you than they would for me. We will each have our own unique formula, which, by the way, is also is likely to change over time.

## Reflection:

*What qualities or attributes are "non-negotiable" and which are you willing to compromise on? (80/20)*

*Have you ever thought something wasn't negotiable but then met someone and were surprised by what you were okay with?*

*Which characteristics or attributes are more or less weighty at this moment in your life than they might have been 5, 10, 20 years ago?*

# LESSON 4: HOW DO YOU KNOW IF YOU'RE COMPATIBLE?

Okay, so now you're really thinking critically about what's important or even nonnegotiable for you in future relationships. But what if you're already partnered and need to look at whether it's truly working for you? Here are some check-ins regarding compatibility and goodness-of-fit for current relationships:

If you feel like it constantly costs you a great deal of energy to make yourself seen or understood by your partner, it might be wise to ask yourself in a very serious way if this is the right relationship for you.

If it's like navigating a minefield to communicate what should be a relatively straightforward thing to your partner, you may want to consider that perhaps you are not well-suited for one another. Or at the very least that you might need to seek some kind of outside help to learn how to talk to each other in a way that doesn't feel so difficult.

If you have said to yourself or others many times that you wish this relationship were easier, but despite your efforts it continues to feel challenging, I'd invite you to consider and honestly critique your reasons for staying in it. *What is this situation doing for you?*

I'm not at all saying you should give up on a challenging relationship without making concerted effort, *if* you think it will be worth it should things smooth out. This is especially true if you're already married, because the assumption when you did so was that it was a lifetime deal. As well, if you have children together, you owe the relationship significantly more effort to make things work than if you don't.

That said, I've said before and I'll say again: you owe the relationship your best efforts, but I do *not* believe people should stay together solely for the kids. You can decide how you feel about this perspective, since I understand many people disagree with my stance. I think that since children tend to do best with happy parents, you actually harm them by staying together unhappily, even if you think you "hide it" pretty well. Kids need to see balanced, happy, *relatively easy* examples of relationships in order to develop a sense of what it means to choose someone else in partnership in a healthy way.

As a culture, we are enamored with the idea of a two-parent household, and while that may be ideal, the truth is there are many different ways to be a family. Forcing a marriage to continue beyond when it can be done well is a bad plan, in my estimation. If you cannot find a way to be happy together, the examples you are setting for your children by sacrificing your well-being for theirs are actually not helpful to their understanding of equity and fairness in relationships. It is not teaching them anything about healthy relationships, which are those where people are together because they choose each other each day, not because they feel stuck, obligated, or beholden.

In this book, I will offer you many opportunities to try new things that might ease up the level of challenge. You might come across one solution that is the panacea *(cure-all)* for your issues. (It could happen!) But I am also quite sure there are many people who are perfectly content with their relationships just as they are, easy or not. However, my guess is that could just be because they don't know for sure that there's a better way. I hope those people read this book and it gives them food for thought.

To be clear, I'll keep repeating my caveats lest you forget or mischaracterize my intentions: I am not at all advocating we all get divorced at the first sign of trouble. There is value in commitment and perseverance, and in weathering life's storms together. I am merely suggesting that we reframe the popular notions that hard work automatically means it's worth it, that a relationship is ever "just how it is," or that all marriages are worth saving.

Every relationship is a dynamic and entirely unique thing, and everyone can benefit and grow from learning new skills. Even if the new skills just mean you are able to end the relationship amicably and with kindness, that's okay. Those skills will translate to future relationships that will hopefully be much easier from the start.

Whether you're single, in a casual dating situation and considering whether to take it further, or if you are open to taking a real inventory of your current relationship, I am gently suggesting across the board that when you're in a healthy, sound relationship, you will simply breathe easily *most of the time*. When you are partnered well, you can communicate fairly easily, and minor misunderstandings remain minor and are easily remedied. The other person speaks your language (or at the very least understands it) and *sees* you clearly. There is a natural flow to the connection. Conflict is done well and with respect, or at the very least, you're always striving to do it better and resolve things more smoothly. There is, at minimum, fundamental kindness to every interaction. It may not be easy all the time, but it's easy*ish*.

If you're interested in such things, which at our core I believe most of us probably are, the ones hallmarked with this ease are the kind of relationships that will sustain you and meet your need to connect deeply. That is a compatibility factor to keep an eye out for: when it just *feels good*.

# Reflection:

*What messaging have you gotten about "working hard" and its intrinsic value?*


*Have you ever been in a relationship with someone who was clearly not a good fit for you? What made you continue (if you did)?*

# LESSON 5: SEX

**M**any *(many!)* marriages suffer from mismatched sex drives. Often, one partner wants more sex than the other, or one partner loses sexual interest altogether *(which does not necessarily mean they've lost interest in their partner)* or the two partners simply like and desire different kinds of sex and cannot easily find a happy medium. Unsurprisingly, sexual incompatibility in any form can cause myriad problems and issues, from resentment to coercion to guilty feelings to reluctant sexlessness to infidelity and the inevitable loss of trust infidelity brings.

But.

What if instead of being upset, ignoring it, cheating on each other, or divorcing, you were willing to get potentially uncomfortable and really dig into the problems? What if you started talking openly about the issues in your marriage and getting creative about how to renegotiate things?

Like, for example, what it would be like to open your marriage up to other sexual partners for one or both of you? Non-monogamy just might be the answer to the issues.

Don't freak out.

Work with me.

Imagine: what would it be like if you stayed together but dated other people? What if one of you said, *"I'm feeling unfulfilled but I don't want to end our relationship. What can we do?"* or *"I don't want to keep turning you down for sex and disappointing you, but I don't really feel very sexual these days. Would you be open to finding someone else to have sex with, while staying committed in our marriage?"* or *"It would really turn me on if we went to a swingers party together and just checked out the lifestyle. We could use some excitement to keep things interesting."*

(Or something like this)

The thing is, it's a lot of work to keep a relationship exciting and fulfilling over a lifespan. And people's sex drives naturally fluctuate. People's needs and wants and desires change. But that doesn't always have to signal disaster. It doesn't always have to mean somebody is going to have to sacrifice or go without, or that the relationship should end.

Here are some other things to consider:

*If non-monogamy is not quite the answer, what about remaining monogamous but trying new things?*

*Have you discussed your deepest sexual fantasies?*

*What about getting some sex toys?*

*What if one of you should see a doctor about your sex drive to see if it's a result of a hormonal imbalance or a side effect from a medication?*

*What if one of you is simply not attracted to the other person in a sexual way? What does or could that mean for your future together?*

*What if one of you has no desire to ever have a sexual relationship?* (Asexuality is on the continuum of normal human sexuality, which can and often does fluctuate and change.) *What would that mean for the relationship? Can you stay together knowing this? Is there room for the relationship to be simply platonic? Could the one who does have active desire have other sexual partners and still maintain the relationship?*

*Would taking sex off the table resolve much of the tension between you? If so, then what can be done to meet the sexual needs of the one who still feels up to or desirous of a sexual relationship? What compromises can be made that will feel good and safe for both of you? Or could it be okay for both of you that you no longer, or rarely, have sex?*

See what I mean? Extreme honesty and vulnerability is required. It can feel awkward at first, but these are the kinds of conversations you can and should be having, regardless of whether your issue is sex or something else. Getting really honest and even pretty uncomfortable can build trust and intimacy. It can even be the first step on a path towards a completely new way of communicating. Once you go there and feel how transformative it can be to be radically honest and open, you may decide you always want to do it this way.

And listen, sexual compatibility *is* important, so you may be unable to find a compromise or arrangement that works for both of you. That isn't ideal, but it might happen. In that case, even if you ultimately decide to end the relationship, if you have really dug into the issues and gotten creative with potential solutions, it will feel like the right decision and it will be okay. Separating will be proactive and not reactive. It will feel less like a "giving up" and more like a mutual and well-earned conclusion you've reached, along the lines of, *"This has run its course"* or *"Let's not do this anymore."* It will feel clear that it's right, even if painful, and will free you both up to find partners (or not) who are a better fit for you, whether sexually or otherwise.

I don't want to understate how challenging it can be to have these kinds of radically vulnerable conversations, so do your best. But if you can't figure out a way to have the conversations in a productive way, get them started with a couples' counselor that you both really like and feel safe with. They can offer you some frameworks for how to do it on your own.

## Reflection:

*What's currently going on in your relationship when it comes to sexual compatibility?*

*How do you feel when you think about making changes in your sex life?*

*If you're not currently partnered, how has sexual compatibility presented challenges in the past?*

*Are there conversations like this you need to be having in your relationship?*

*What keeps you from having them?*

*What might happen if you just go for it?*

# LESSON 6: "INFIDELITY"

I would estimate that at least half of the couples I see in counseling come to me as a direct result of infidelity. They want to rebuild and repair the relationship after the betrayal of one partner stepping out of the relationship. It's generally just as messy regardless of "what kind" of infidelity, whether it was a sexual relationship or "only" an emotional affair.

The complication is that rarely is the so-called "infidelity" (I don't love this word) *just* about sex or emotional connection. Usually it's about needs, whether clear or convoluted, whether expressed or unexpressed, that aren't being met in the primary relationship. Don't get me wrong, sometimes it's merely about opportunity and novelty, which is still obviously The Wrong Thing To Do, insofar as it violates your agreements, but maybe doesn't have deep emotional roots. Maybe it's not an indictment of the relationship in that case, but an expression of boredom or desire for something new. Either way, all of these make a mess. All of these situations could probably have been avoided with some radical honesty.

Now, this does not mean it's ever the fault of the person who got cheated on, just that these things can be more complicated and nuanced than, *"They are such a jerk for cheating."*

*(Of course, sometimes a person is a serial cheater because of unresolved wounds or some other dysfunctional reason, or maybe they're truly a jerk, and either way, that's a different situation. Couples' counseling is likely not the solution in this case.)*

Years of counseling couples through these situations has led me to wonder: *Why does this happen so often? What's the thing? What is the appeal of cheating?* The "cheater" nearly always feels ashamed and guilty when they are caught, because they really don't want to harm their partner. Ironically, they usually don't even want to leave the relationship. Or sometimes the cheating happens because the relationship has been over a long time but neither party is ready to call it quits yet. Often, they have children together and a shared life that is important to them both. And yet, they do it anyway.

This is especially frustrating when the partner who was cheated on asks incessantly, *"Why did you do this?"* and the person who stepped out doesn't really have a clear answer. I have come to understand that sometimes there simply *is not* a clear answer, which is deeply unsatisfying to someone who just wants an explanation in order to make sense of things and begin to move forward. Sometimes the answers are layered in to the very history of the relationship, and so to explain "why" would mean to go back through all the years and excavate everything. It would mean exposing lots of old cracks in the foundation that they may have been ignoring or patching over for a long time. Sometimes people don't even know where to begin doing this work, so they just shrug and say, *"I don't know why I did it."* And it's kind of true, but the whole truth is much messier than that.

Okay, so how can people keep from having affairs and causing so much pain to their partners when things get boring or difficult, or when sex drives aren't in alignment, or one person has needs the other can't or won't meet? How can people remain "faithful" to the agreements they've made to each other?

I mean, you could say, *"Well just don't cheat! Be faithful! Suck it up. You agreed to for better or worse."* You *could* say that, but I certainly won't. I simply don't believe it is that simple; furthermore, I think a reductive approach like that does everyone involved a disservice. People are so much more complex than a one-size-fits-all Relationship Rule about Monogamy and The Right Way to do it. Remember: *there is no right way to do relationships.*

My best guess is that radical communication is the most effective key here and that people being willing to get uncomfortable and extremely vulnerable with each other early in the relationship would eliminate much of the suffering "infidelity" causes, simply by rendering it a less useful tool. What I mean by this is that people often use other people or situations to meet a need they have not adequately expressed to their partner. If people were able to just talk about what's really going on with them, they might find that they can collaboratively create a positive solution, rather than finding a negative one for themselves. Because if you think about it, cheating is a solution of sorts, it just isn't a very good one in terms of, you know, healthy relationships.

An important piece of the conversation about "infidelity" is the very concept of monogamy, which is the idea that one person can or should be able to meet your needs forever. You may not have resonated with these ideas in previous lessons but let's just keep talking about it, okay? Even if you've never one time considered anything like what I'm about to say. Just have an open mind and hear me out.

Over the past few years, one of the many things I have begun to realize is that monogamy actually isn't a good fit for everyone. As I previously mentioned, I actually think that if monogamy *-as a hard and fast absolute rule-* was eliminated from the relationship equation, I'd probably see far fewer couples in therapy for so-called "infidelity."

Because, generally speaking, I think it is unreasonable to expect one person to meet all of your emotional, sexual, intellectual, social, and spiritual (etc.) needs. Expecting or requiring monogamy in all of these areas from your primary partner over the course of a lifespan, if we're assuming "marriage is forever," is nearly always setting yourself up for disappointment. You have to be able to get some of your needs met outside of your intimate primary relationship. Being radically honest about what those needs are is crucial, even if that ultimately means being non-monogamous in one of the categories that we stereotypically expect couples to practice monogamy.

Namely, I'm referring to the sexual and emotional.

For example, in terms of emotional monogamy: if you "allowed" each other greater freedom to have intimate friendships -yes, even with the gender(s) you are attracted to- there might be fewer "emotional affairs" whereby someone is ostensibly trying to get their emotional needs met in the "wrong" way. Remember earlier when I said that the best relationships are those in which each partner feels free? Contained within that notion of freedom is the right to determine for yourself, in a respectful way, what makes you happy, and the agreement that you should be able to seek that happiness out. Of course, this requires tremendous amounts of communication and trust.

So, what if instead of reflexively agreeing to arbitrary restrictions, you were radically honest about what you really wanted the relationships to look like? What if you were like, *"Okay, so I love our relationship in these ways but I don't love it in these other ways, so I need to have meaningful relationships outside of ours in order to feel fulfilled. That might mean sharing intimate information and/or quality time with a person (or people) other than just you. Let's talk about it."* And what if your partner was able to hear that, understand it, and not frame it as a rejection of them? Do you think you could hear this from your partner without framing it as a rejection of you? It is decidedly *not* a rejection, but it can feel like one, so you'll have to navigate each other's feelings carefully and talk through everything.

People often instate "rules" about who their partner can and can't be friends with, which, by the way, is the exact opposite of allowing our partners to feel free. So, for example, opposite sex friendships for straight married couples are often just totally off the table, under the guise of, *"It's just not what you do when you're in a relationship,"* or a flat and unsupported, *"I don't like it,"* or a shaming, *"It's weird."*

I hear my clients saying things like this all the time. Things like, *"I used to have a lot of _____ friends before we got married, but, you know how it is."* I don't let them off the hook with this. I might say something like, *"I do know how a lot of people choose to live, but I'm not sure it's actually a rule that you can't be friends with whomever you want to be. What do you think?"* Honestly, the idea that you are expected to give up your friends in order to make your marriage work is bizarre to me. I would certainly never agree to it, especially since many of my dearest friends are people I could theoretically be attracted to, and in some cases, have actually dated or been intimate with in the past. *(Gasp!)*

I understand that refusing to allow your partner to have certain friends is an attempt to limit temptation, but there are so many problems with this approach. First of all, it's a backwards notion that people can't have intimate friendships with people they could *potentially* be attracted to without being "disrespectful" to their primary relationship. Being attracted to someone in some way doesn't automatically mean you're going to sleep together or that you'll ever even let on that you're attracted to them. It certainly doesn't guarantee that anything untoward will ever occur.

It's also an old and unhelpful idea that there is actually any way to control your partner into not cheating on you. Furthermore, it's totally unreasonable to expect that there is actually any way to eliminate all so-called "temptation." A human out in the world is going to encounter all manner of other humans they may be attracted to. Frankly, the more you try to restrict most people, the less happy they are. The less happy people are, and the more controlled they feel, the *more* likely they are to stray. It's counterintuitive at best to try and control who your partner is friends with *(or what they do, what they wear, what they share on social media, or who they talk to)*.

Aside from the controlling piece, it is also important to frame "monogamy" as encompassing more than just sex. Mono means one. One partner. To approach our relationships as though *monogamy in all ways* is the norm suggests that one person could possibly be the source of all pleasure, satisfaction, stimulation, and so on in someone's life. Expecting this sets you up to fail, because it's basically impossible. It can wind up putting extreme pressure on a relationship that might otherwise be relatively healthy.

To be clear, monogamy works just fine for some people, depending on their needs at this particular stage in life. Some people have no interest in (or energy for) more than one partner. That's fine. I actually understand this as well. I'm introverted, have a small child and limited energy to share with other people, so having another whole relationship to navigate doesn't appeal to me at all right now. But for me, to have the *option* and the *freedom* to be able to discuss it with my partner is crucial, regardless of what I actually do. In my case, it's a principle more than a practice, and I think it's important either way to have *"does monogamy work for me/us?"* be part of the conversation.

I also don't want to insult the efforts of people who have decided on sexual monogamy, stuck with it, and ultimately found it satisfying. Some people enjoy the dutiful nature of monogamy, and intentionally frame "making sacrifices" by limiting sexual partners across the lifespan as one of the things that makes the marriage feel like a real commitment. I can understand that, too.

And of course, some people are very traditional, have internalized cultural messaging about relationships, and would never feel comfortable even *thinking* about doing things differently. I honestly mean no disrespect to those folks, but they probably aren't my target audience. But for those of you who are committed to living into your highest and best self, and having the healthiest and most satisfying relationship(s) possible, these ideas may shake up your notions of what it means to be in relationship with others. Some changes may become necessary. These specific ideas may or may not impact how you move forward, but it's possible they would give rise to your own ideas about what will specifically work for you, and *that is a good thing.*

All of this said, I don't think there is a magic solution that will free every relationship from the risk of "infidelity," but making a couple of tweaks to our accepted conventions will help. First, I encourage you to re-conceptualize the framework that assumes, as a default, that most people's needs can be met by one person. Secondly, you need to continue to stretch your communication to include all the things you're currently not saying.

# Reflection:

*When you think about "infidelity," what comes up for you?*

*Have you ever considered "monogamy" to be problematic in your own relationships?*

*Do you agree with my premise that "infidelity" could (at least sometimes) be avoided if people felt more free in their primary relationship?*

*What do you think about the idea of emotional non-monogamy?*

# LESSON 7: FRIENDSHIP

*"There is nothing on this earth more to be prized than true friendship."*
—St. Thomas Aquinas

Frankly, I think we've all been duped when it comes to what we "should" be looking for in relationships. After years of observing couples (and living through my own messy dating history), I have come to believe that successful "dating" and eventual partnering is about finding someone who matches your intensity, whatever it may be. I don't think it's about traditional compatibility factors like, *"We both love to camp and hate country music!"* but more like, *"We prefer to connect at a similar level."*

Hear me out: to some people, regularly engaging in deep and meaningful conversations about existence, the universe, and the meaning of life is the pinnacle of happiness. But try pairing that person with someone who's like, *"Ugh why is everything so SERIOUS all the time,"* and see what happens. (Spoiler alert: nothing good, usually.)

The thing is, it doesn't matter if they both love all the same movies and music and TV shows and travel destinations and vote the same way and even share fundamental values. Their *intensity* levels are mismatched and misaligned and they probably will never find deep happiness even though on paper they have "everything in common." They actually have profoundly different preferences when it comes to how, when, and in what ways to communicate. *(If you're into MBTI®, this may refer to differences between Intuition and Sensing preferences.)*

Furthermore, deep friendship is more sustainable than sexual chemistry. Sexual compatibility is important to varying degrees, depending on how necessary sex is to your happiness. However, if you're looking down the line to a long life together, you're probably better off partnering with someone who is a dear companion. You hopefully also enjoy having sex with them, but there is likely to come a point in life where sex is less interesting than it once was. For most people, however, a desire for friendship and connection never ages out.

On that note, here are some tips about partnering well:

Partner with someone whose company you truly enjoy, because at some point you may not be able to do too much besides just be together.

Partner with someone you can be comfortably silent with. There may be a time when just sitting and looking at the world is all you feel like doing.

Partner with someone you love to have conversations with, whose perspective you appreciate, and whose wisdom you seek.

Partner with someone who is kind and generous, because there will be times when you are sick or sad and will need to be able to completely rely on the support of your mate. Having a person by your side who will take care of you and accept your care in return is invaluable.

Partner with someone who makes you laugh and who gets your jokes. Laughing is crucial to happiness.

Partner with someone who "gets" you and sees all of you. Someone who lets you grow and change, because changing and evolving with age is inevitable. Partner with someone who understands and expects this.

Partner with someone who grants you grace during times of conflict.

All of this is to say: make a choice based on rational criteria when it comes to your life partner. Choose a person based on criteria that has longevity. The things you want, desire, or enjoy today may not always be the same things you ultimately need over your lifespan in order to be content.

So the person with the perfect body who looks a certain way, or the person that makes a ton of money but is somewhat vacuous, may be satisfying enough to you right now, but their looks and body will change, and money is cold comfort at best. As such, those are probably not the best predictors of long-term happiness. The meditation: throw your vision down the tunnel of time and see what the relationship could look like in 10, 20, 50 years. What changes can you predict? How satisfying does it look the longer the life together?

Honestly, the main reason I think my husband and I will stay together for the rest of our lives is because we have a deep and sincere friendship at the core of our relationship. Sex is great, but it isn't our main thing. Our main thing is that we sincerely like each other and enjoy being together. The key to this relationship is that we accept one another fully, and we encourage and expect growth and change. We actually don't have many of the expected "compatibility factors" in common; that is, we don't really like to do many of the same things. But we laugh together, enjoy talking with each other, co-parent beautifully, forgive each other easily, and share values about what we want our family to be like. It feels sustainable, healthy, and most of all, it is relatively easy. Our other needs can be met through our individual activities as well as through other relationships, for which we give one another space, trust, and freedom. *It really works*. I am writing this because I want this for everyone.

As I've alluded to throughout these previous lessons, it's taken me a long time to arrive at a place like this; I've taken many detours on the way. If I were my own therapist, this relationship feels like the first place I'd advise myself to stay. I see in this relationship the qualities I tend to observe in the couples I've worked with who stay together and would self-report happiness, even after a hiccup. Because remember, going to counseling doesn't signal disaster; it just means you are seeking help to get through something. The stronger the friendship, the more likely you are to successfully navigate challenges when they come up.

# Reflection:

*Do you agree or disagree with my theory that friendship is the most important factor in partnering well?*

*Have you experienced a relationship in which the person was your best friend and favorite person? What did it feel like, or what do you think that might be like?*

*If sex was the only thing keeping you together, what happens if things stop "working" or someone loses sexual desire?*

*If money was the thing, what happens when a job or the ability to earn is lost?*

*If x was the only thing keeping you together, what happens when x is removed from the equation?*

# LESSON 8: USE WORDS

*"Much unhappiness has come into the world because of bewilderment and things left unsaid."* — Fyodor Dostoyevsky

I see many couples who present with the generalized complaint: *"We just don't communicate well."* This nebulous complaint of "not communicating well" can take many forms, from literally not understanding what the other person is saying, to responding defensively to every perceived criticism, to just not talking much at all.

Not understanding each other could be because of style difference. For example, perhaps one person is extremely literal and concrete, and the other uses a lot of metaphor and analogy, and communicates abstractly or conceptually. Neither is "wrong," but it simply means neither is using a communication framework that is easily translated to the other. The person who is extremely literal may take in everything the other says as though it is actually solid and well-thought out *information*, as opposed to merely pieces of data. The more abstract communicator may actually not be transmitting information at all, but may just be trying on ideas out loud, and resent being held accountable for every word they say. This is actually a very common issue that is sometimes relieved simply by naming it and making sense of it. (If this names your issue, it can probably be accounted for using the MBTI® framework and identifying a difference in Sensing vs. Intuiting preference.)

The next communication issue I commonly see: defensiveness. Responding defensively is always harmful to relationships. That said, it is a natural consequence of feeling like you are being misunderstood or criticized, so when the relationship has suffered from years of struggle, it makes sense that it would be hard not to get defensive. Learning to bypass the other person's defensiveness is the main key to effective conflict resolution. (The appendix of this book contains many strategies to do this, so definitely refer to it for specific tips.)

Not talking at all could be out of fear of saying the wrong thing, not really knowing how you feel, or maybe just lack of emotional vocabulary. What I mean by that is maybe you don't know what to call how you're feeling or how to make someone else understand it. Or maybe you used to try to communicate, but it never felt like it went well, so you gave up. Regardless of the iteration, the results are the same: one or both partners are left feeling unheard, disconnected, and alone in the relationship, often for years on end.

You can assume then that failure to effectively communicate eventually lends itself to myriad other issues. Feeling unheard over time leads to simmering resentment and feeling uncared-for. It can also lead to active conflict when trying to make your partner understand, as well as stonewalling when you feel like it's just not even worth bringing up (but you're still upset). Eventually, the relationship may suffer from complete emotional disconnect.

Sadly, it is often the case that people just never learned *how* to communicate effectively. Perhaps your parents, peers, and/or previous partners also did not know how to communicate. This is common; if you'll recall, I have already acknowledged that most of us are not well-trained in How To Do Relationships. Thus, acquiring even the most rudimentary communication and conflict resolution skills makes a radical difference and empowers couples to avoid many of these common issues. Because if it's your situation that you and your partner just *do not communicate well,* I am here to enthusiastically inform you that you don't have to live like that. I promise. Communication is a skill, and you can learn it the same way you have learned to do everything else you know how to do.

Think about learning to drive a car. If you're anything like me, when you first started driving, all the things you had to think about at once felt overwhelming and stressful. You had to be very intentional and consciously aware about pressing the brake or the accelerator, and thinking about *okay which one is the windshield wipers and which is the turn signal and oh no it's starting to rain and ugh up ahead is a left turn across traffic*...and you probably made a ton of mistakes. Your parent or teacher probably white-knuckled their way through many a drive with you behind the wheel.

But think about driving now. (I'll wait while you try.)

It's actually kind of hard to think intentionally about driving because, like...what is there to think about? You just *know how to drive*. As an adult, you've gotten so good at driving that it's natural. We go whole moments on autopilot while driving where we literally don't think about what we're doing, or where we are headed, because our muscle memory just knows. You simply get in the car and do the things that make the car go where you want it to, and then you arrive. Little to no conscious thought is required most of the time, right?

I am excited to inform you that if you do the work and practice, even when you're not that good at it yet, even if you're clumsy and awkward and fumble around a little bit, *eventually* communication can be a lot like driving a car. You will just know what to do, and it will go pretty well, and you'll get where you're trying to go. And by being a good communicator, you will naturally mentor the people around you and help them become better communicators as well. There will be far fewer "accidents on the road," as it were.

This sounds elementary, perhaps, but I literally created a class called "Use Words" *(parenthetically referred to as "Say What The F\*\*\* You Mean")* because I learned after a few years as a counselor that most people have *no idea* how to effectively communicate. For a lot of folks, it is a struggle all the time, but it becomes especially challenging when they feel vulnerable or emotional. We'll work on it together.

## Reflection:

*How would you assess your current communication skill level?*

*What have you learned over your lifespan about your own challenges when it comes to communication? What gets in your way and what do you find pretty easy?*

*Think about relationships that feel easier or harder due specifically to how you each communicate. What do you think might have made a difference?*

*Do you think it's true that learning to communicate more effectively will naturally result in easier, happier relationships?*

# LESSON 9: DON'T BE PASSIVE-AGGRESSIVE

\<full stop\>

J ust, don't. It's an easy trap to fall into and you may often reflexively do it, but it does nothing positive for your relationships and, in fact, is one of the very worst ways to communicate. I personally have to make a conscious effort to not be this way, and it does take a lot of mindfulness to keep from defaulting to it. But because I spend so much energy defying my instinct for the benefit of others, I personally have very little patience for other people behaving passive-aggressively towards me.

If you recognize yourself as someone who is frequently passive-aggressive, it would behoove you to get started on your recovery, because *I promise* nobody likes it when you do that. If you have something to say, just say it. Don't make people dig it out of you or do a bunch of extra work to clarify how you're feeling and why. It is much easier to resolve conflict, or avoid it altogether, when you are being direct.

First things first, though, while I assume everyone has heard of passive-aggressiveness, not all of you may feel clear on what it actually is. People ask me about this a lot, especially in couples counseling, so here's a basic dictionary definition:

**\*\*pas ·sive-ag ·gres ·sive (adjective): of or denoting a type of behavior or personality* *characterized by indirect resistance to the demands of others and an avoidance of direct confrontation.* \*\*

In other words, it is a way of avoiding using your words to express how you actually feel and instead going about it indirectly to try to get the same point across. You may do this because it gives you an "out" if it's ineffective, so you can later claim that the other person misunderstood or misread. You may do it because you like to keep things "light" and so passive-aggressiveness feels like a way to be funny or non-confrontational and still get your sharp little dig in. In my experience, people who readily say they're "sarcastic" are usually just passive-aggressive; they are often hypersensitive, but wrap their sensitivity and reactivity up in "jokes" so they never have to own it or work on it.

In the spirit of offering grace, I'll say that most passive-aggressive communication seems to actually be about avoiding vulnerability. It tends to happen when you don't feel entitled to or capable of more directly expressing yourself. Of course, it can feel a little bit scary to say that you're hurt or upset, especially if you aren't certain that your feelings will be received well or attended to. I talk more about vulnerability in other sections of the book, but the solution as it pertains to passive-aggressive communication is to do some work to get more comfortable with vulnerability. The more comfortable you are, the more readily you will be able to own your feelings and state them directly, rather than make people work so hard to understand where you're coming from by making it convoluted and effortful.

**Examples of passive-aggressive communication:**

- Saying, *"It's fine"* or *"I'm fine"* or *"I'm not upset"* when *clearly* it is not fine, you are not fine, and/or you are mad/upset.

- Intentionally waiting or failing to respond to something you know someone is waiting for you to reply to.

- Taking an unnecessarily long time on something in order to communicate that it is not important to you.

- Comments like, *"Oh I see how it is!"* or *"Forget it"* or *"Don't go to any trouble"* are often passive-aggressive.

- Intentionally messing something up or making it overly complicated to avoid having to do it instead of just saying "no".

- Backhanded compliments.

In all of these cases, you are communicating by not communicating or by intentionally mis-communicating or misleading. You are not actually saying what you mean, which is confusing. Some things to consider if this is your habit:

*How is anyone supposed to connect authentically with you if they don't know how to take what you say or do?*

*Do you know how much work it is to undo conditioning that has taught people not to trust the word of other people because they're so used to passive-aggressive behavior?*

The thing is, it doesn't benefit you to use this method to communicate. Say you are obviously upset, and the person you're upset with asks, *"Hey, are you okay?"* Here is your opportunity to get the attention you want! They are asking you to tell them what's going on. So now what is the point in claiming, *"Yes, I'm fine"* if you're clearly not? Anyone who is either very literal or has grown impatient with your passive-aggressive behavior is likely to shrug and be like, *"Okay, good,"* and move on as though you are fine. Because you did *say* you were fine.

You don't then get to be mad that the person doesn't respond to your feelings.

YOU SAID YOU WERE FINE.

Sorry for shouting in all caps, but this is terribly frustrating to observe and is so unbelievably common. You *want* the person to know they've harmed you and made you upset, or else frankly, you'd do a better job of hiding it. So here we are: they can see and feel that you are upset, which is why they asked in the first place. They are demonstrating that they care about your feelings and are giving you a chance to describe what's going on. Maybe you don't trust that they will handle it well if you tell the truth. But instead of using the opportunity to even attempt to resolve the issue, you actually make it worse by lying.

That may feel harsh. Maybe you never thought about it as being dishonest; perhaps you were just trying to avoid conflict, which you've been socialized to believe is "bad." Maybe you think you're just being a peacekeeper. But here's another way to think about it: denying the emotional energy someone can see and feel from you is a form of gaslighting, whereby you cause them to doubt their own assessments. Secondly, you're literally lying, which always erodes trust in relationships. Thirdly, and perhaps most importantly, you don't actually get what you want, which ostensibly *is to feel better.*

So how about you skip all the extra steps and just say, *"Yes. I am upset. It is not fine. It hurt my feelings when you did x thing."* And then move directly into resolving the issue. It may be messy, but at least it will be honest. What would that be like?

Years ago, a client offered me the most amazing acrostic. I use it frequently when trying to help clients undo their conditioning of saying it's fine when it's not fine. Think of "Fine" in this way:

**F**eelings
**I**nternalized
**N**ot
**E**xpressed

It is rarely in the best interests of your relationships to deny your feelings, especially when you are offered an opportunity for resolution. I have a rule in my personal relationships and I always tell people this, explicitly, *"I will never tell you I'm fine (or it's fine) if I don't mean it. You never have to wonder if I'm secretly mad at you. If I say something is okay, you can trust me."* Do you see how much easier that makes things?

Here are some more specific tips about passive-aggressive communication:

- Don't withhold communication.

- Don't be intentionally hurtful just to get back at somebody for hurting you. Tit-for-tat doesn't work in healthy relationships.

- Don't *not* respond to something you know a person is waiting for you to respond to just to make a point or to leverage power.

- Don't pay backhanded compliments.

Here is a real life example: *"I don't usually like tattoos, but yours aren't bad"* is a thing many people have said to me, and it's annoying. It's not actually a compliment, because you passive-aggressively let me know you disapprove of the tattoos in the first place. To make this a sincere compliment, you'd just say, *"I like your tattoos!"* I've also received the same fake compliment about having short hair, like, *"You're cute even though your hair is too short."* I'm sure most of you can think of times someone "complimented" you and it actually made you feel badly. Backhanded compliments are annoying because they don't actually leave the person feeling like they've been complimented. It feels gross. Stop doing it.

- Don't say things like, *"I see how you are"* or *"I see how it is"* if what you're really saying is, *"I'm seeing you do something for someone else that I want you to do for me"* and don't say, *"Don't go to any trouble"* if what you mean is, *"Would you please go to this trouble for me?"*

- Do be direct about asking for what you want.

- Don't use "guilt trips" to try and get people to do what you want rather than just ask outright.

- Don't expect people to read your mind.

- Communicate clearly, directly, honestly, and often. Even if it's awkward and you feel vulnerable doing it. It's *way better* than working so hard to get your point across through all the back channels that everybody is annoyed and tired at the end.

As an aside, there are many memes and jokes about women being passive-aggressive, and I do think that's fair, to some extent. White women, in particular, are often socialized to be "nice" at the expense of being "honest." This results in many of us being extremely conflict-avoidant. And what happens when you prioritize politeness over honesty? You get passive-aggressive, "nice-nasty" behavior in which displeasure is expressed indirectly. This results in white women coming across as two-faced, duplicitous, gossipy, etc. when I think it's probably more accurate that we are uncomfortable with the possibility of conflict and will go to great and inadvisable lengths to avoid it.

That is not meant to suggest that other women don't also rely on passive-aggressive communication, and it is *certainly* not to say men or nonbinary folks don't either, just that the reputation for this behavior from white women is culturally well-earned and easily observed.

It seems like people socialized as men tend to use passive-aggressiveness a little differently, more often by withholding information or emotional response. This may be because they are socialized not necessarily to avoid conflict, but more specifically to avoid vulnerability and emotional transparency. Men who are very sensitive often show up as extremely "sarcastic" (which is actually passive-aggressive), because they don't know how or don't feel entitled to express how frequently their feelings are hurt. The extreme end of this is anger and even violence. Remember that people will go to great lengths to protect themselves, whether from real or potential harm, and this definitely includes emotional harm.

I could probably write a whole book on passive-aggressive behavior, to be honest. Most of us are guilty of it, to greater or lesser degrees, so if you recognize yourself in this lesson, don't feel too bad. You're in good company! It's an easy trap to fall into, and vulnerability is hard, especially at first. Commit to doing the work to get more comfortable expressing yourself directly so that you can stop making people jump through endless hoops to decipher how you really feel or what you want. Model this effort so that other people want to emulate how well you communicate.

Personally, I love and appreciate the people in my life who are direct and honest with me. I value the people who say when they're not fine. I appreciate if when I ask, *"Do you need anything?"* and they say, *"no,"* I can trust that they aren't secretly mad at me for not doing something I didn't know they wanted or needed done. I love knowing that I have at least a handful of people I can count on to not be passive-aggressive, and when I accidentally default to passive-aggressive behavior they can call me out, or I can call myself out and apologize. Your relationships will definitely benefit from working on this.

# Reflection:

*How did it feel to read this lesson?*

*Which parts did you recognize yourself in?*

*If you find you rely on passive-aggressive communication on a regular basis, are you able to identify your reason behind it?*

*Did or does your family of origin rely on passive-aggressive behavior to communicate?*

*What did this teach you?*

*How can you start today to make some adjustments?*

# LESSON 10: DON'T DO REAL CONVERSATIONS VIA TEXT

A nother tip about communication from my "Use Words" class is this: when at all possible, try to avoid having meaningful conversations via text message. A few years ago when I taught this class the first time, I literally printed out copies of screenshots from a friend's text conversation with the guy she was dating and distributed them to the class. (With her permission, of course!) We used the screenshots as samples of all the things that can go wrong in text.

I had the group pair up and take notes, with the assignment to identify all the opportunities the couple had to repair the connection. It was powerfully informative. You could see where in one place, she tried to de-escalate and make a repair attempt that he missed. In another place, she was passive-aggressive and he took the bait. He name-called and she cursed at him. It was a whole mess.

The main takeaway is that texting makes it too easy to be cruel as a reflex. They were nasty to one another in ways I doubt they would be when speaking in person. The triggers that you may be able to manage in real life can sometimes be too tempting in text, when the person's face isn't there to refer to.

Let me say this all a different way, and sorry for shouting at you again but this is important: TEXTING IS NOT A GOOD TOOL FOR MEANINGFUL

## DIALOGUE OR RESOLUTION OF INTERPERSONAL ISSUES.

It's convenient, true. I hate talking on the phone, so I don't begrudge anyone a preference for texting over talking. I definitely get it. And it's great for, *"Hey what do we need from the grocery store?"* It's ideal for me for scheduling clients. Lots of people have developed a preference for texting over other means of communication. Dating apps make texting the default for initiating conversation with a love interest.

That said, a "preference" for texting is a slippery slope because it's also a seemingly safe and easy way to say stuff you might be too shy or feel too vulnerable to say out loud. It lets you avoid the very things you need to be practicing; you are learning how to be vulnerable and take risks and basically just *use your words*. Right?

Texting is not conducive to relationships, in general, but *especially* do not use texting for conversations where anybody is anywhere in the vicinity of anger. The problem is that it's too easy to say stuff in the heat of the moment and then quickly press send and feel vindicated. The speed with which you are able to escalate via text doesn't honor your relationships at all. It potentially gives you like three seconds of satisfaction, but then in the time it takes the other person to receive it and respond, you've already typed out something else. Next thing you know, you're having parallel conversations about nothing, not actually responding thoughtfully, and just being harmful to each other without having to take responsibility for the impact.

Seriously, let me say that again slightly differently: it is virtually impossible to communicate clearly via text. So why do we insist on carrying on deeply personal, important conversations this way? Text messaging allows you to heedlessly toss words at each other without taking proper time to craft what you are trying to say, as you would in a letter, for example. *(I would much rather have people write letters to each other than use text!)* It also costs you the option of managing your message in real time as you see, or hear from their inflection and tone of voice, how it is landing on the other person.

There is so much room for error from both the sender and the receiver, and such profound lack of nuance that I'm amazed any relationships that rely heavily on texting even survive. I really think that the only real means to effectively communicate in a way that is productive, concise, and respectful is to speak to one another in real life, preferably in person. Face-to-face communication will always yield the best results.

## Reflection:

*What do you think about texting and communication?*

*How does texting play into your relationship communication?*

*Are there things you would say via text that you'd find challenging to say, or would never say, in real life?*

*What do you think might change if you eliminated the option of using text for meaningful discussion?*

# LESSON 11: TELL
# THE WHOLE TRUTH

Tell *your* whole truth, whatever that may be, no matter how uncomfortable it makes you or whomever you're telling it to. Tell it even if you're not proud of it, or you think your partner won't get it. In order to have a relatively easy relationship, you have to be someone who can be trusted to communicate truthfully, clearly, and in a timely fashion. In other words, don't sit on a frustration for days or weeks and then bring it up in some other context. As you learn to tell the truth in real time, you will also model this for your partner so they will feel safe doing it with you.

What I've consistently observed in couples' counseling is that the story of the relationship is fundamentally different for each partner. You each have a unique "truth" when it comes to nearly every single interaction, and neither is exactly right or wrong. You simply see and interpret things differently. The story of the relationship and what happened in a specific interaction is always filtered through your own lens. It is inevitably colored by your past and is reactive to the wounds inflicted by that past. In my work with couples, I always assume that the "truth" in any objective sense is somewhere between your versions of the story.

The secondary factor to this mismatch in "truth" about things is the fact that nobody seems to ever tell each other the actual whole story. Invariably in couples' sessions, I'll ask, *"Did you tell her that it hurt your feelings?"* or *"Did you tell him how that made you feel?"* or just *"Did you say that?"* and the answer is almost always, *"Well…no."*

??????????????????????? (<—That's a symbolic rendering of the face I make.)

Remember: YOU CANNOT BE MAD WHEN YOU DON'T GET WHAT YOU DIDN'T ASK FOR. You know? So if your partner doesn't know they are upsetting you or hurting you or pissing you off, you can't fairly hold them responsible for it. No matter how much you think *they should just know.* This is always the response, too, that they should *just know.* Well, clearly they do not, because presumably, if they knew, they would change or work on it.

Now, if they really do know and they still don't do anything different, well, that's a different story and you can claim legitimate grievances. But even in that case, I'd suggest approaching with curiosity if you're able to muster it. Try asking what gets in their way and keeps them from making greater effort to meet your needs. Or if they believe they are making effort, but you still aren't seeing anything changing, talk about that. There is typically some sort of explanation or story that emerges when you are willing to have these conversations. I'm not saying the answer will necessarily be satisfying, but at least you'll understand their perspective a bit better, rather than just having a blanket assumption that they're not even trying when in fact, they may feel like they are.

The practice is to work on expressing your truth in real time. Verbalize your expectations, since a great majority of conflict is borne of mismatched (and often unspoken) expectations. Say out loud what you want, need, desire, and fear. Even if you don't like doing it. Even if you're scared. Even if, like one of my clients, you have to literally hide your face because you can't tolerate how vulnerable you feel. That is okay. (And it will get easier.)

Make an agreement to keep up with your partner about what the "true story" of the relationship is in real time. Check in periodically: *"This is how I'm experiencing our relationship (right now? recently? always?)…How does it feel to you?*

*Is there something we need to change?"* Get on the same page regularly so that the "truth" is approximately the same for you both, even if your interpretation is slightly different. It is crucial that you be operating inside the same relationship so that when it comes to resolution, you don't first have to waste a ton of time coming to agreement on what has even transpired so far.

So if something happens that lands on you in a particular way, say, right then, *"I didn't like how that felt. Can you say that differently?"* or *"Here's what I just heard you say, is that what you meant?"* And so on. Yes, these are skills. Yes, they take practice. Yes, you can do it. Yes, you can ask your partner (or other loved ones) to practice it with you. Yes, you can teach them. The next lesson will help!

## Reflection:

*Think about times when you and your partner have seemed to be existing in different relationships. What helps (or has helped) you to get on the same page?*

*Think about times you have been reluctant (or outright refused) to share your "truth." What got in your way? How can you get past this resistance?*

*Are you doing anything that may be shutting your partner down from being able to share their whole truth with you?*

# LESSON 12: DOING CONFLICT WELL

*"When you say something really unkind, when you do something in retaliation, your anger increases. You make the other person suffer, and he will try hard to say or to do something back to get relief from his suffering. That is how conflict escalates."*
— Thich Nhat Hanh

Another class I developed is called "How To Do Conflict Well" *(aka "Don't Be An A\*\*hole")*, which is essentially a giant list of tips and tools for how to fight fairly and not be a jerk even when you're mad. (See Appendix for full list.)

The key to doing conflict well is understanding that conflict, in and of itself, is not inherently bad or scary. It doesn't signal disaster and it doesn't suggest that the relationship is over. Having conflict doesn't mean that you're a bad person, or that things will never be okay again if you "go there."

In fact, like it or not, conflict is an important component of a healthy relationship. No one agrees perfectly with another person at all times; it is inevitable that sometimes you will disagree and have to compromise and come to new understandings. In order to form those new understandings, you typically have to move through all the stages of conflict in order to arrive at resolution. *This is fine, normal, and to be expected.* It just has to be done *well* in order to not cause lasting harm, so skill-building in this area is crucial.

The first and arguably most important tip I can offer for doing conflict well in your intimate relationships is to do your very best to enter every difficult conversation with the idea held clearly and firmly in your mind *that you love them*. Because, of course, if you love a person, you do not have any desire to harm them. In fact, in a calmer moment you would probably say you'd willingly do whatever was required to protect them from harm. Right? You would stand up for them and fight to keep them from being hurt.

Keep that same protective energy when you're engaged in conflict. This includes holding their best interests and safety in mind *even when you believe they have harmed you*. Even when you feel it is grossly unfair for you to have to do any emotional heavy lifting or apologizing.

I say this regularly in couples' counseling: it may be unfair sometimes, but you cannot keep score. Sometimes the person who is harmed or has a legitimate grievance has to step up more than they think is reasonable in order to move the relationship forward. I call this "emotional heavy lifting" and I am the first to acknowledge that it is a big ask. But if you truly love a person, and the relationship is generally healthy, reciprocal, and worth saving, then you know you lose nothing when you apologize first. You lose nothing when you take the first step, because your priority is resolution, not retaliation. In a healthy relationship, it is also safe to assume that the balance of emotional effort is equalized over time, so if you have to work harder *this* time, you can trust that they will be the ones to work harder next time.

If you love a person, this includes taking no pleasure in making your loved one cry or in saying whatever cruel thing you can conjure up to ensure they end up feeling as badly as you do. So if you're someone who tends to throw verbal daggers when you're hurt, I would invite you to do some real work on that and learn to retract your claws and take deep breaths before engaging. Remember that you cannot take back things you've said, and that every instance of conflict done poorly erodes the quality of the relationship.

I get it, this whole lesson is a struggle for a lot of people. Even after years of teaching this class, it can still be challenging for me as well. If I'm being honest, my default settings for conflict are not great and do not produce desirable outcomes! Doing conflict well takes a lot of practice and sustained effort. You may have to spend quite a while consistently practicing this before you feel like it starts to improve in any measurable way. It may feel especially daunting when you realize that you should probably start practicing this in all of your relationships, not just your intimate partnerships.

Part of the challenge to doing conflict well is that when you are in a really sad, hurt, or angry place, it can seem nearly impossible to muster up positive intentions towards even your most beloved intimate partners. But it is crucial that, even in painful situations, you are able to maintain a position of *unconditional positive regard*.

If you'll recall, I talked about this concept earlier in regard to relationship to self. It is foundational to healthy relationships in general. It should also extend to everyone with whom we are in any kind of meaningful relationship, at all times, not just romantic ones. It basically means that whatever you do, I will still fundamentally respect you as a person and treat you with decency. It notably does *not* mean "to love unconditionally," (which I actually don't think is even realistic anyway, except in the case of parent-to-child love.) In other words, I can treat you with unconditional positive regard, even when we are in conflict, and simultaneously accept that maybe this relationship isn't right for me or I don't want to be in this situation.

So, treating each other with decency, even in conflict, is key. But it's also important to bear in mind that conflict, when done well, is about catharsis. It's about saying what needs to be said, clearing the air, and excavating the truth so that you can find a way to move forward and let go of the problem once it's solved. If there is no clear solution to be found, then it is about going forward comfortably once you meet at a compromise you can both live with.

It is notable to emphasize again that it is *not an inherently negative thing to have conflict.* Some incredibly healthy relationships can contain a fair amount of conflict, especially when you combine two strong personalities or throw people into particularly challenging circumstances. The problem isn't the conflict itself. The problem is when conflict consistently turns into ugliness, which results in erosion over time. Done well, however, conflict lends itself to a series of new understandings and agreements regarding how the relationship works best for both of you. This will inevitably lead to less conflict over time.

That said, if you simply can't talk to your partner in a particular moment without being ugly, I would invite you to use my favorite phrase and say, *"I love you too much to have this conversation right now."* Or, once engaged in conflict, one or both of you might want to remind the other, *"Don't forget that we love each other."* Whatever it takes to be able to hold in your mind that you, first and foremost, love this person and wish them no harm will radically change the way you do conflict.

Practice this: *"I love you too much to have this conversation right now."*

Using this sentence will buy you a little bit of time to get your internal house in order and figure out how to proceed productively. The only rule is that you do have to actually come back to the conversation; you can't use this and then just move on without resolving anything. It's not a getaway car!

Another key to effective conflict resolution is to not feel compelled to make the other person suffer, and to really step back from needing to do that. If you have to, step back and stay back until you can return to the situation in peace, with the intent to reconcile. You may have to actively remind yourself over and over that you are safe, conflict is not bad, and that conflict arises as a natural reaction to some discomfort or disagreement.

Most conflict is borne of misunderstandings. Often, it arises from unspoken expectations that your partner failed to meet, at least in part because they were never expressed. Most of the time, when you have a conflict with a person, if you sit down and look at their face and ask questions and listen to the answers, you will be able to resolve it peacefully and even (relatively) painlessly. It is rarely as bad as you fear and it's almost never worth avoiding.

Moreover, you will often find that you were entirely mistaken in how you perceived the other person's actions. Often, they were likewise entirely mistaken in how they perceived yours. But how regularly, instead of getting curious about what just happened, do you have a miscommunication or a confusing interaction and then just run with your anger or irritation at the person who made you feel bad? Worse, you then assume or even decide something about them based on whatever annoyed or hurt you.

What you end up with is being angry or hurt over something the other person may not have intended or even realized was bothering you. If you don't say something along the lines of: *"I didn't like when you did this. It bothered me. Can you tell me what you were thinking or feeling when you did this?"* Or *"Help me understand what happened here,"* and then actually listen to the response, then you can't expect true resolution to whatever the conflict was to begin with. You will just make up a story about it and carry on as if your story is true.

If you don't say anything, if you do not investigate and get curious, you have effectively agreed to let a relationship suffer or a connection die because you took something personally, made assumptions, and didn't have the courage to examine it. For me, the best relationships I have in my life are the ones where I know that whatever happens, we will:

a) Talk about it

b) Work through it collaboratively

c) Commit to forgiveness

d) Agree not to punish each other for past transgressions

This is an "agreement" we have made over the course of the relationship; we have agreed that the relationship, whatever it is, whether love, friendship, or family, is important enough to treat carefully and to approach courageously, to ask questions and to avoid assumptions. The relationships where this is par for the course are the ones that I value most. They are the ones I feel the most safe, accepted, authentic, and connected.

*(Throwing in my caveat again about abusive relationships in which the balance is never fair and the victimized partner always does the emotional heavy lifting. This is not okay and this is not a relationship that is "generally healthy, reciprocal, and worth saving." I am not suggesting that if you are in a dysfunctional or violent situation that you are responsible for doing more work. You are responsible only for doing your best to keep yourself safe.)*

## Reflection:

*Which of your relationships have similar agreements in place, whether implicitly or explicitly?*

*Which ones tend to suffer from misunderstandings?*

*Is it you or the other person that tends to make assumptions or avoid asking the hard questions?*

*What can you do differently?*

*How can you approach your loved ones from a place of curiosity, even when you're triggered or hurt by their behavior?*

# LESSON 13: RADICAL GRACE

U sing what I call "radical grace" can also help frame your approach. It is essentially the benefit of the doubt, granted freely and without condition. It is the willingness to assume neutral or positive intent in the absence of information. Basically, being willing to admit that you don't know what happened exactly, and you know you don't feel good, but you aren't in a hurry to blame it all on your partner.

Because oftentimes, when you are upset with someone, it is probably accurate to say you have gotten there without much *actual* information. You often apply your own meanings, leap to conclusions, and then act as if your feelings are facts.

So radical grace means defaulting to curiosity, asking, *"What did you mean by that?"* or *"Can you say that a different way?"* and leaving open the possibility for you to have been mostly or entirely wrong about how you received something. It also gives them space to try again and not have their feet held immediately to the fire for something they may have clumsily stated or mistakenly done.

It is the practice of remaining neutral and open, instead of leaping to your go-to assumptions like, *"As usual you are trying to hurt me."* It means not looking for reasons to be hurt or upset, but instead defaulting to the assumption that your partner is not trying to hurt you, despite the fact that you may, in fact, feel hurt. *(Assuming your partner is a kind person in general, and that in a calmer moment you do believe they don't have intentions of harming you.)*

It is hard. As I've said before, I still struggle with this stuff sometimes. In my relationships in general, when I am upset or hurt, sometimes I want to just hold on to my feelings and disconnect. Sometimes I want to just be mad and not do the work.

In my marriage, sometimes I want to punish my husband. Sometimes I want to just walk away from a hard conversation, go to bed mad, and withhold forgiveness or reconnection. But I know that won't help me to build the relationship I want. And if I'm being honest, I actually do trust that he really isn't *ever* trying to hurt me. I know that he loves me, is a deeply kind person in general, and certainly doesn't wish me harm. But once I go down a bad-feeling rabbit hole, it can be really hard to drag myself back up to the surface to remember that my feelings are not facts and that I need more information.

Radical grace is taking a deep breath, getting back up, and going back to your person, saying, *"That hurt my feelings"* or *"I'm sorry"* or *"This is what just happened for me; can we talk about it?"* and trusting them to meet you there with an equal offering of grace.

It really is hard to hold yourself to the standard of always being willing to forgive, able to let go of perceived slights, and quick to extend the olive branch. That is way outside the parameters of a typical way of approaching conflict, whereby you "lose" if you give an inch. You have to be able to hold the idea that there is no individual "winning" in a healthy relationship. There is only the relationship and its success or failure. An analogy I used recently with a client went like this: Imagine you're playing a game of CandyLand and you have one playing piece, your partner has one, and the relationship has one. Each time you or your partner advances alone, your relationship loses a space. Pretty simple concept, right? The key is abandoning your individual playing pieces and focusing collaboratively on moving the relationship itself forward.

I know it's a big ask. This is a very different way of doing conflict than most of you are probably used to. I understand that it's hard to risk the vulnerability of saying, *"That hurt my feelings,"* and asking your partner to do something to make you feel better. But if both of you are regularly practicing it, they *will* do something and it *will* make you feel better. Radical grace is freedom. Everybody wins, because the relationship itself wins.

# Reflection:

*When you think about using "radical grace" in your relationship, how does that feel?*

*Are you someone who typically resists giving grace or who holds on to perceived slights for a while?*

*How do you think your relationship might benefit from a shift in this direction?*

*How might you begin to practice this principle?*

# LESSON 14: APOLOGIZING WELL

pologizing well is one of the greatest gifts I can give to myself and my relationships. Not only people I know and love, but also the other people in the world at large. Learning to recognize when I've done or said something harmful and immediately attempting to repair any damage I've caused with careless words or actions is critical to being in relationship with others. Being willing to humbly ask forgiveness for mistakes is not a sign of weakness. It means you're willing to be accountable for yourself.

Here's the thing: you're never going to be as awesome as you intend to be. Your words will come out in ways you don't intend them to, and you'll sometimes (probably) be an asshole. *That is okay and to be expected. You are human.*

Definitely work on not making the same mistakes repeatedly, but in the meantime, learn to apologize well. It can be hard on the ego, so for those of you who are very prideful, this may prove difficult. But it's worth the effort, because this is how we build and stabilize, or in some cases, rebuild and re-stabilize, relationships. The key is being accountable to each other by apologizing readily.

One of the ways I practice this is with my daughter, who, as of this writing, is four years old. I am quick to apologize to her if I jump to a conclusion, or if I snap at her, accidentally cause her pain or hurt, or if in some way I just don't live up to my own standards of parenting. Likewise, I am teaching her about telling the truth, owning her mistakes, and apologizing when she causes harm. We practice it together.

Here is an example of how that looks with her. I might say, *"I'm sorry I snapped at you; I was feeling frustrated, but I shouldn't have used that voice with you. Do you forgive me?"* Likewise I'm teaching her to say things like, *"I'm sorry I hit you when we were playing; I was playing too rough and I didn't mean to hurt you. Do you accept my apology?"* We practice saying, *"How can I make it right?"* after an apology. I do not let her just reflexively throw a half-hearted "sorry" at me, and I don't do it to her. We address the questions, *"What are you sorry for? How do you plan to make it right?"*

If you have children, I suggest you begin teaching them how to apologize, and to forgive, well. We do this pretty naturally now, and it makes our relationship that much healthier and stronger. My hope is this lesson will frame how she behaves in her relationships as she grows up.

My husband and I have started doing this as well, as there is much opportunity to apologize in any long-term relationship. I'll admit, it's more often me who owes apologies in our house. I can be sort of prickly sometimes; I get irritable and snappy when I'm tired. I can be critical. On the other hand, he is generally pretty even-tempered and unlikely to snap at me or be hurtful, but I'm also more sensitive than he is.

And things do happen, of course. Just the other day, I was annoyed with him for something, and was on my way out the door to head to work when it happened. He texted me a few minutes later and said, *"I'm sorry for what I did. I know you don't like that, and I won't do it again."* At first I just texted back *"Okay. Thanks."* But then, as so often happens in this work, I remembered my own teachings and realized I owed him more than that. So when I got to my office, I texted again and said, *"I accept your apology."*

Adding, *"I accept your apology"* or *"I forgive you,"* may sound weirdly formal to you, but I believe it is a crucial step in reconciliation and forgiveness. It is a way of making it clear that we are okay now and the issue is over. It is imperative that once forgiveness is offered and we've wiped the slate clean, we won't have to revisit whatever the event was. It is a way of sincerely acknowledging the apology.

Just saying *"okay"* in this context is actually a mild form of passive-aggressiveness because it was via text so there was no way for him to really know if it was sincere. (I admitted previously that I have a little reflexive passive-aggressiveness in me!)

Now, I want to make sure to clarify that just apologizing all the time for, like, everything and nothing *(for just existing or taking up space)* is an unhealthy habit that a lot of you are probably in. I see this frequently, especially in people who've been socialized as women. Many of us have been taught by our culture to shrink and hide and apologize constantly. People of all genders who are in the habit of people-pleasing may over-apologize as well, as a way to make sure nobody ever has cause to be upset with you.

If this resonates, this lesson is not for you *just yet*. Your pre-work, before you even begin to work on apologizing well and with intention, is gaining clarity on *when you actually even owe an apology*. Next is making sure that you are clear on what, precisely, you're sorry for. Your concurrent work is continuing to interrupt your habit of apology-as-reflex.

Let me say this clearly: You owe no one a "sorry" for your existence, your voice, or the space you occupy.

While I'm at it, let me say this also: Don't apologize for your body, either. Your body is nobody else's business. That's a whole thing in itself that unfortunately many people wrestle with, especially when navigating gender expression, or when trying to be a healthy bigger-bodied femme person, but I'm here to tell you: you are just fine how you are. *(If need be, go back and revisit the lessons about loving yourself and being kind to yourself and that you're beautiful just how you are.)* You owe no one an apology for freely and openly being who you are.

That was a bit of a tangent, but I felt like it was important to say all of that about reflexive apology and people-pleasing. Okay, back to regular programming.

Now, of course I always forgive my kid, but things might look different if I were having a conversation with an adult who apologized to me. If the wounding act was egregious and I was still feeling too hurt, it is also entirely acceptable to say, *"I am not ready to forgive you yet, but I think I will be soon."* (Or something like that.)

If you're able to accept it, certainly do so. But in the interest of authenticity and being able to trust each other in ongoing relationship, I would encourage you to not accept an apology for any reason except that you sincerely forgive the person who has wronged you. You don't "owe" anyone forgiveness. I believe in restorative justice, but I don't believe in compulsory forgiveness. That said, if you're ready to offer forgiveness when requested, it can be profoundly healing.

I will talk more about forgiveness in another lesson. Meanwhile, let's also talk about *how* to apologize since you may be interested in being better about apologizing but need some direction to hone these skills. No worries, most of us will have to intentionally learn this at some point!

### First, here are some examples of how *not* to apologize:

- I'm sorry you got upset/you were offended/etc. (The *"Well actually, it's your fault"* apology)

- Well, excuse me! (The defensive apology)

- My bad. (The non-apology apology)

- I'm sorry you didn't understand what I said. (The *"I didn't actually do anything wrong"* apology)

- I'm sorry you found out about that/I'm sorry I got caught (The celebrity apology)

**In order to apologize well, it is helpful to:**

- Understand and express, fully and sincerely, that you understand why the other person is upset (e.g., *"I totally get why you're upset about that."*)

- Ask questions if you don't understand (e.g., *"Can you explain to me exactly what I did or said that bothered you so that I know moving forward?"*)

- Take ownership of what happened (e.g., *"I'm really sorry I did that."*)

- Explain, but don't defend. (e.g., *"I truly didn't mean to hurt you; my intention was..."*)

Most importantly, don't do the same thing again. Some people think that if they apologize every time, it makes up for the fact they keep doing the same thing. However, your apology eventually becomes rote and won't be accepted as sincere. To the person you're apologizing to, it'll just sound like the same old excuses. They have no reason to believe you're actually going to do anything differently.

The key to apologizing well is to be willing to be accountable for your words and actions, as well as proactively making the necessary adjustments to ensure the problematic behaviors don't continue. You want to know how you can make it right. This is how you demonstrate sincerity and intention.

# Reflection:

*What is your usual relationship to apology?*

*If you're someone who struggles to apologize, what gets in your way?*

*What do you think might change if you started practicing apologizing and used some of these skills?*

*How does it feel when someone sincerely apologizes to you? Is it hard or relatively easy for you to accept it?*

# LESSON 15: DON'T HOLD GRUDGES

*"Holding on to anger is like grasping a hot coal with the intent of throwing it at someone else; you are the one who gets burned."* — Buddha

I know a guy who carries a lot of emotional baggage around with him, namely in the form of grudges he's holding. He has a running list in his mind of all the people who have done him wrong, in all the different ways, over his entire lifespan. Most of his friendships and familial relationships are struggling or have ended, and yet he doesn't connect to the idea that *it isn't that surprising* considering he has basically just been taking inventory of all the things that have pissed him off or hurt him.

In my observation, he has either forgotten or simply failed to put forth effort into developing the good aspects of these relationships. He doesn't seem to notice when anyone in his life does kind or loving things, because he is hyper-attuned to being let down. *(Google the term "hostile attribution bias" if you want to know what I think is going on here.)*

Notably, he doesn't take any degree of responsibility for the condition his relationships are in. He is convinced that they are all just selfish, harmful, thoughtless people…which to some extent, they probably are. We all are, or can be at times. However, it seems like people are especially inclined to be that way when someone meets you at the gate with the expectation that you will let them down or harm them. When you feel like you are starting at a deficit, it makes it really hard to climb back into someone's good graces. It feels impossible, daunting, and not worth the effort. Most people will eventually just give up.

What I tried to explain to him is that these same people are probably also giving, loving, thoughtful, and kind as often as they aren't. But that they are more likely to be that way when they are in relationships with people who expect them to be kind and loving, and who approach them with kindness, love, grace, and most importantly, forgiveness.

I've suggested to him, and I'll suggest to you now as well in case you need to hear it: how about instead of assuming everyone is going to let you down, maybe just assume the people you're in relationship with are mostly good, but also mostly unaware of their impact on others. Like, maybe they will let you down, but they probably didn't mean to.

So if it's someone who matters to you, and you generally believe them to be a decent person, practice not taking it personally when they aren't always perfectly good. Maybe even try to forgive them, unasked, when they make what are obviously just mistakes. Remember, my definition of radical grace is *"offering the benefit of the doubt, freely and without condition."*

Practice letting go of the small things that you *could* take personally and get hurt by, and choose not to. If you believe in your bones that the person isn't intentionally trying to harm you, it does nothing positive for the relationship if you insist on punishing them for every single misspoken word or thoughtless action.

If there is one thing I've learned about humans it is that most people, at their core, are fundamentally decent. Let's just say that generally speaking, people either don't realize or seem to care how they are coming across. They are only thinking about how they themselves feel, and actively trying to protect themselves from pain or discomfort. Most people have huge blind spots, especially if they have been hurt in the past or have deep unresolved trauma. Fear can also make people very tunnel-visioned and self-absorbed, and there is a lot of fear energy circulating our culture right now. This definitely contributes to people not being at their best.

So if you accept this, then the best thing you can do to radically improve your relationships is to forgive the people you love when the slights are small, and to consciously recognize and reject that lack of awareness in yourself. Begin really paying attention to your impact on those around you. Remember that we often criticize in others what we dislike in ourselves. Start tuning in more actively to how others might be feeling if that hasn't always been part of your interpersonal repertoire.

But don't stop there. This is an active process: also give your loved ones constructive feedback, and ask for it in return. Teach people how to treat you. Show where your boundaries are and maintain them. When you are hurt, say, out loud, some version of, *"I don't like when you do that; it hurts my feelings. Can you please do it another way?"* and give the person an opportunity to treat you how you'd like to be treated, instead of getting angry or hurt and refusing to offer absolution or resolution.

Often, people just don't know they are hurting you, and how would they? You didn't tell them, or maybe you told them, but in a passive-aggressive or aggressive-aggressive way that they were unable to hear behind the defensive screen they put up to protect themselves. It's a vicious cycle of hurt and disconnection.

For some reason, we seem to find it very satisfying to be righteously angry with people for the harm they have caused us. But generally speaking, the satisfaction of holding a grudge is fleeting, and not worth it. So my advice is always to use words. Tell people how they have affected you, and get curious about how you have affected them. When someone informs you that you have hurt them, move into collaboratively envisioning how things could look different and feel better between you moving forward.

Remember, like it or not, there are always two sides to every story. How you "read" a situation is often vastly different than how the other person "read" it. But until you sit down and discuss it, you won't have the details of the other person's experience. Practice radical grace and forgiveness. Don't hold grudges.

**Principles of Radical Grace and Forgiveness:**

- Assuming we all have work/growth to do

- Allowing yourself to grow

- Assuming the best of intentions in others (benefit of the doubt)

- Approaching with curiosity when someone disagrees or challenges you

- Seeking to understand, first and foremost

- Sincerely asking for forgiveness when you make a mistake

- Offering sincere forgiveness when it is requested

- Bypassing defensiveness

- Recognizing the shared goals and win/wins

# Reflection:

*What is your relationship to grudge-holding?*

*If you are someone who struggles to forgive, what is that about?*

*Do the principles of radical grace and forgiveness appeal to you?*

*How do you think they might affect your relationships, if you were to adopt these principles?*

# LESSON 16: LONG-TERM FORGIVENESS

You married folks out there, a lot of this will be for you, because long-term relationships have their own struggles. Based on my professional experience, it's probably safe to assume a lot of you are probably deep-angry with your love partners, and may be struggling with this section of the book. If you've been together many years without the skills to resolve problems and issues, this is even more likely. Radical grace may seem like a wild concept, and that's okay. You have to start where you are.

Maybe your situation is that every time you fight, you feel compelled (or justified) to dig down in your sack of ancient hurts and pull out something your partner did ages ago and hurl it at them. Maybe that feels like what you have to do. Maybe it's an old habit and you don't know what else to do. Whatever the motivation, the problem is nothing ever gets resolved because every fight is ultimately about old shit. It doesn't get a chance to be about *"the thing you just did that isn't that big of a deal,"* it more often devolves into some *"you never"* or *"you always"* accusation, which really just boils down to: *"I feel hurt."* Or maybe, *"I have felt hurt for a very long time."*

The interesting thing about this is that when I probe to see if a person who does this a lot wanted to let some of it go, they panic a little bit. Think about it. What would it be like to let all this old stuff go and forgive your partner? Does that feel hopeful or terrifying? In some cases it's almost as if all that righteous anger provides some measure of comfort. It's almost as if you wouldn't know how to be together without it.

I think it's like this: if you are not historically and justifiably angry with your partner, then you may find that what you are left with underneath that is a profound sadness or loneliness in your relationship. And because sadness is much more uncomfortable than anger, you may continually choose to be angry instead because then it is always their fault and because then you don't have to feel vulnerable. (That V word again!)

Perhaps you are not quite ready to end the relationship, for any number of reasons, but you are likewise not willing, or don't feel able, to take another step forward. You don't want to ask for something and risk the rejection of not getting it. You may have done this many times before and been disappointed.

If you're angry, you don't have to try and teach your partner how to treat you and have them fail or, worse, not try. You may feel like you have tried this too many times already. You don't want to risk feeling sad, rejected, or disappointed again. And so you get to just be mad at them instead, which also doesn't feel good, but it's safe. You understand this feeling. You withhold forgiveness because this alternative state of habitual anger is easy and comfortable, albeit rather miserable.

Does this sound familiar to you? Frankly, I know a lot of people in relationships like this, to varying degrees. People who one might describe as having that proverbial *"chip on their shoulder"* in a specific relationship (or all their relationships). People who are denying forgiveness to others because being angry and resentful and hurt feels safer or more comfortable than opening themselves up to the possibility of being hurt again.

First, lest I risk disingenuousness: I do get it. I completely understand the attraction of keeping score, building walls, and holding grudges. Being vulnerable is scary, and disappointment feels awful. Full stop. I don't blame you for wanting to avoid it and try and keep yourself safe.

But, I also believe that a grudge will provide cold comfort, at best. You actually won't find happiness here in this closed-off state. Furthermore, I believe that true intimacy, vulnerability, and trust, as well as the building or rebuilding of a meaningful connection, is pretty much always worth whatever forgiveness costs. Which is not to say that forgiving your partner automatically means the relationship is healed. You may forgive them and still decide to end things, but you will at the very least free yourself from the weight of that anger you've been carrying.

So, my advice is to do some deep digging, unearth all your emotional dirt and muck, and take an inventory: *are you carrying around a bunch of stuff you don't need? Are you withholding forgiveness for some reason? If yes, do you even know what the reason is or is your grudge merely an historic precedent at this point?*

*Are you a person other people struggle to get close to because you're always quick to anger and slow to forgive? Or does someone else need to meditate on this so that they can heal and move forward, or so that you together can heal and move forward?*

Look, it's a lot of work to stay mad. Grudges occupy an inordinate amount of emotional space. It feels like a literal burden. Learning to release that feels like freedom. Although, sometimes you don't know or won't trust this until you do it and feel lighter and then you'll say, *"Man, I wish I'd done this sooner!"* Yes, of course it takes work to make a big shift as well, but it's not the sustained effort of grudge-holding.

An even better plan is to avoid the buildup in the first place. If you are able to exorcise all the old demons from the relationship and forge a way forward, then the next step is to learn how to express how you feel and offer space for the other person to express how they feel. *The key is to do this in real time.* No holding on to things that are inevitably going to slip out passive-aggressively later anyway. Learn to forgive the small things without being asked, and to offer the benefit of the doubt. Again: practice radical grace. Granting the people you love grace feels good, kind, and loving, and moreover, it creates space to have more healthy and positive relationships in general.

For that old stuff: if you and your partner cannot seem to undo your old patterns, take inventory of your current feelings about it. Namely, do you *want* to do the work required to heal your relationship? Or, would you both be happier if you ended this effort and went your separate ways? (This is not a wrong answer!)

Next question is, if you do want to do the work, can you agree to go see a counselor to help you do it well? In the process, you will hopefully agree to avoid letting things building up again in the future. The key then is to excavate and heal the past, move forward in a positive way, and commit to not repeating the mistakes. The key is grace…and a really, really good therapist that you both feel safe and comfortable with. Stick with it. See the counselor regularly, for months or even a year or two, and then keep that therapist on deck for future issues even once you "graduate." Things will inevitably come up, but once you have better skills, you can use your skills and resources to get ahead of them.

I would also suggest that you endeavor to accept all sincere apologies as a standard practice, assuming you are ready to genuinely forgive and reconnect. It can also be helpful to begin to recognize repair attempts, even when they are subtle. See and acknowledge the ways your partner tries to reconnect with you. When possible, be willing to let go of whatever animosity or anger you may feel, even if you believe it to be "justified." It is a lot of work to hold yourself to these standards, and it probably won't always feel fair, but it's important to remember that true and generous love doesn't keep score. Clear the old dirt away and see what's left. Forgive. Heal.

# Reflection:

*Which parts, if any, of this resonate with you?*

*What are the hurts you're holding on to in your relationship?*

*What would it be like to release and forgive them?*

*Which parts of this lesson might be hardest for you?*

# LESSON 17: NEED IS NOT A GIFT

*"Be careful when a naked man offers you a shirt."* — African Proverb

When you enter into a romantic relationship with a person who holds profound unresolved trauma, is unhealthy in some significant way, or simply does not believe themself to be worthy of love, the most common end result is that you become responsible for their emotional well-being. Even if you also have "issues," which frankly, most people have, you become a source of strength and a "need" for the person. *(That "need" can sometimes look a lot like addiction. Addiction, co-dependency, and lack of boundaries all occupy the same relational space.)*

In an intimate relationship, this is an inherently imbalanced and unhealthy dynamic insofar as it is a crutch that allows a person to continue walking around without a shirt on, to extend the metaphor. Any "love" this person offers is not sourced from a place of genuine well-being, so to some extent it simply cannot be trusted. When a person who does not love themself says, *"I love you,"* it can be translated to something more akin to *"I love that you make me feel better about myself"* or *"I need you in order to feel whole"* or maybe *"Thank you for loving me, because I do not know how to love myself."*

In both my work and personal life, I observe people doing this all the time. It seems true that some people are just attracted to "projects" or else have given up the hope that there are even healthy people out there. In my own life, I have certainly had a type. In the past, close friends often referred to my type as "broken birds," because I always seemed to be doing a lot of repair work in my relationships. In my defense, I will say the people I have loved who may fall into this category were and are amazing and wonderful people. At the time I found them, they just really needed someone to help them or "see" them. I felt like I was the one for the job, and it gave me some degree of satisfaction to provide love and support.

Sometimes it's hard to tell at first if someone is a "broken bird," but it is evident once you look closely. However, because it is intertwined with all the wonderful and human things about them, you are able to see them in all their potential. You may feel compelled to help them heal. You respond to their need, and it usually doesn't feel bad at first. This need will be particularly attractive, whether consciously or unconsciously, to those of you who are emotional givers and healers. *(It also rather conveniently allows you the option to focus on their issues and avoid dealing with your own. Just saying…)*

Sometimes you don't even consciously know that that is happening until you are full-on In A Relationship. To a lesser degree this can happen in a friendship as well; it just tends to be more evident and less distressing when a friendship is imbalanced. Friendships can naturally drift apart; you don't always have to "break up." There's usually less drama in those drifting-apart scenarios.

In an imbalanced intimate relationship, you may feel like you are the best thing for this person. The notions, *"I'm the only one who really understands them"* or *"But they need me"* can be extremely compelling. Feeling important is attractive. And it may not feel like it is actually costing you anything because you do this so naturally. Maybe you like to be useful, and so responding to a person's need feels productive and comfortable.

It may honestly feel like you're doing something good, but in these scenarios, you ultimately do both yourself and your partner a disservice. You are selling yourself short by investing in someone who simply hasn't the capacity to love you back fully because they haven't learned to love themself yet. There's no real opportunity for balance in this dynamic. Furthermore, you are enabling the person you care about to use your love as a crutch to prop them up and provide them with a sense of worth that is external to them. A person's sense of worthiness has to be found within if their love is to be sourced sustainably.

Unfortunately, *this is not work you can do for another person.* However, you can show them that you believe them to be worthy of love and you can love them fiercely. That is profoundly healing. Too, you can demonstrate loving yourself, which may include having hard boundaries. I want to be clear that I'm not saying a person with deep wounds isn't worth loving. I am merely saying you cannot fix people or make them get healthy. You cannot resolve another person's trauma. You cannot make someone else happy; our best and highest work in relationships is to facilitate one another's happiness, not be its source. Need is not a gift.

I know this is one of the hardest lessons for those of you who feel it is your duty and obligation to take care of others. It was a hard lesson for me, too. But this relationship mantra has to resonate fully in order to move past your tendency: *"It is not my job to make you feel better about yourself. Neither is it yours for me."*

The best way to have a healthy relationship is to meet at the intersection halfway between your own respective self-loves and self-awareness (or if you are earlier in your development, your own *desire for and effort towards* self-love and self-awareness). Of course there is space to grow, and no expectation of perfection is reasonable, but the greatest and most fulfilling intimacy will be found when you are both whole and both bringing your full, best, and most authentic selves. You will be most satisfied when you want rather than need one another. Or, another way to put it: when you both have your own shirts on.

So your work is to get to know, love, and accept yourself in all your unique glory. Only a person who feels comfortable in their own skin, fully and authentically, and is a whole person on their own, can feel truly comfortable in vulnerability and intimacy. That is how you get the shirt you walk around in.

I talk about vulnerability in a lot of different contexts, but in this case, vulnerability is when you know there's a chance it won't work out, but you do it anyway and allow it to unfold. It is hard. It is not safe or certain. It requires risk, and you have to be not only courageous but also strong. I will always advise you to explore vulnerability, because it's where the magic is. But I also invite you to be mindful of where and with whom you're practicing it. Calculated risks in this context means opening yourself up to someone who feels, and hopefully really is, healthy and whole.

Someone who wants you in their life not because they need you but because you are good to each other and make one another's lives more satisfying is a person worth investing in. That tells you they are willing to take a risk and be vulnerable to the relationship. However, if you feel "needed," there's probably some issues going on. If, when you take a real inventory, it turns out you are doing most of the work to make them feel secure and remind them of their value, but they aren't doing much of that for you, there is a strong probability that there is some unhealthy or codependent stuff going on in the relationship. Likewise if you feel like you "need" each other; it's not ideal.

In my opinion, "feeling needed" should probably be on your dealbreaker list, and not one of the potentially amendable ones like vegetarianism or "must like cats." This may require a lot of attention from you to shift and reframe, and that's okay. Do that work so that you are able to feel the difference between want and need.

You will also want to be able to clearly articulate the idea that need feels like a burden to you, whereas want or desire is a gift. It is helpful to make sure your partner knows that you don't want or desire to be needed, because they may not have any context for understanding this. They may believe that people in love "needing" each other is the hallmark of a good relationship. They may have never seen a healthy relationship up close, and thus have no idea what to be striving for. *(Remember that interdependence is the healthiest state; revisit the lessons about Boundaries if this still feels convoluted to you.)*

The thing is, if someone "needs" you, it should be a clear indicator that they are not a healthy person on their own. That said, note this caveat! If, when you bring it to their attention, they willingly recognize, *"Oh you're right, I do have serious issues I should work on,"* and they start therapy or whatever other healing work they need in order to develop better skills because they want to be healthier *for themselves*, they might still be worth the investment.

So for those of you who are very literal: note that I am saying that the presence of this dynamic doesn't necessarily mean *"throw the whole relationship away"* so much as it means *"be cautious, be intentional, and communicate about what you're experiencing."* Most importantly, always make sure you don't agree to stay in a situation where you feel stuck or obligated, which are the hallmarks of "need." Make sure you both have shirts on.

# Reflection:

*What aspects of this lesson resonate with you?*

*What do you see as the difference between "I need you" and "I want you"?*

*What is your relationship to "broken birds" and dating folks with unresolved trauma?*

*How does the idea of "having your own shirt on" feel to you? Do you have your own shirt on?*

*In what ways do you think loving (or not loving) yourself impacts relationship dynamics?*

# LESSON 18: DATING WELL

This section could also be called *"Dating On Apps Because This Is Apparently What We Are Doing Now."* I rarely meet couples anymore who didn't meet online in some capacity. Personally, I did a lot of online dating (what I guess would be more accurately called "app" dating now) prior to settling down. It's where I met most of the people I ended up dating in my 30s, whether short- or long-term. I tried a lot of different apps and sites. Now, I know these apps are constantly changing and that in the years since I settled down, things have morphed. So some of the specifics of this advice may become obsolete as the style of apps and the ways people use them changes, but I think the advice can easily translate to dating well, in general.

I originally created my list of tips for a workshop I taught several years ago about "How To Do Online Dating," in which we curated photos and brainstormed best practices for profiles. It was super fun, but it seems like people aren't using the apps that require whole written profiles anymore; most profiles seem to basically just be a series of photos. Not too much need for a whole workshop around that. I'm glad it could be repurposed here, because I do think dating is a bit of a lost art.

First and foremost, be YOU. Make sure that your photos, bio, quotes, and whatever else you may have on your profile all reflect an authentic version of yourself. You don't have to disclose everything up front, of course, but if what you're interested in is connecting with another human on a meaningful level, you have to present yourself accurately from day one. Few things feel more uncomfortable in the online dating world than to discover upon meeting someone in person that they are not at all who/how they presented themselves. To me, the greatest compliment one can give or receive in these endeavors is, *"You are exactly the same in person."*

In my dating life, I heard this a lot from men, generally in a surprised and appreciative way. This leads me to believe many other people are not presenting themselves super accurately. So...be YOU, always. The right person is going to like you for exactly who you are. Also, remember that keeping up a façade is a ton of work. Who has the time or energy?

To that end, put only recent photos up, unless you clearly indicate in the caption what is different now or in what year the photo was taken. Most of us do not look how we looked ten years ago, for better or worse, and so to present yourself as a younger or thinner or more fashionable version of yourself is false advertising, which you want to always avoid.

If it's all you have, go ahead and put a group shot up if the people in it are comfortable with it. Have a pal take a normal-looking photo of you that isn't in the gym or bathroom mirror. Use one of your professional headshots if you need to. One or two selfies is fine, but I would advise you not have a whole series of them and nothing else. Make sure at least one photo is a full-length one so that people can't assume you're trying to hide anything.

Write about *yourself* in your profile. Don't just talk about what you want or don't want in another person. Give the people reading your profile information about YOU. What do you do for fun, for sport, for entertainment? Where do you like to go? What are some interesting quirky facts about you? What are your favorite things? (Work talk is generally not super interesting unless what you do is either unique or somehow inextricably linked to who you are.)

Whatever you end up saying, think of it more as a personal resumé and less as a "help wanted" ad. State who YOU are as clearly as possible, and a person who is looking for someone with your qualities and attributes is going to express interest. That said, most of the current apps don't provide much space to write about yourself, so this might apply more to the initial conversations. Once you match and start talking, then you can share this information.

On that note, don't write your whole profile or waste your initial correspondence bashing all the people you've encountered so far. Talking about catfishing and whatnot or making threats like, *"You have to do ____ in order for me to even talk to you."* Don't litter it with endless *"Don't be ____"* and *"Don't bother messaging me if ____"* and *"No games"* and negative or defensive stuff like that.

Make an effort to sound like you're actually excited to meet new people. That's why you're on the sites in the first place, right? So make sure you appear to be open to it actually happening instead of constantly poised to defend against imposters or expecting to be lied to or manipulated.

For the record, I went out with a fairly large number of people over the years. Aside from that one elaborate con I fell for, every single person was who they said they were. Most of them looked like their photos. It's not as common as you might think to be faked out by people in real life. That said, if you *have* been hurt or tricked, I totally understand that and can obviously empathize. However, if you aren't able to engage online without being reflexively defensive, and I say this ever-so-gently, you may need a little more time to be ready to date again. It is really important that you're actually ready when it happens. Otherwise you may end up ghosting someone cool, or being cagey and hard to read, or some other undesirable outcome.

Some sites don't require "matching" prior to messaging, so if someone messages you unsolicited and they aren't someone you want to talk to, just don't respond. That's totally acceptable. You don't have to explain why you aren't interested. If they start bothering or harassing you, block them.

Be prepared to report them if necessary. But whatever you do, don't feel bad for not responding to unsolicited messages. Online dating shouldn't feel like a part-time job or a whole slew of new obligations. You don't owe anyone anything except to be respectful and honest when you do interact with them. You don't have to reply to say you're not interested.

That said, you can reply to every message if you want to, of course. I'm just saying you don't *have* to, and you don't have to worry that you're being rude. Straight men in particular have been known to get ugly when women reject them, so sometimes it's better or safer to just ignore and not engage. Personally, my policy was always to reply if the message was particularly kind or thoughtful, because I did appreciate the time and effort the person took to craft a message to me.

Similarly, if you "match" with someone, start talking with them, and then (absent of some clear reason) decide you're not interested, my personal opinion is that it is rather unkind to just "ghost" *(disappear)* or unmatch them without a word. People do it all the time, so don't feel guilty if you've done it before without thinking too much about it. It does seem to be part of our current dating culture; I just wish people would disengage in kinder ways, especially if you've been talking with them for a bit, have shared some information, and they weren't rude or nasty to you. It's fine to just not be into someone. *"Everything ain't for everybody,"* as my husband would say.

The problem with ghosting is that it can make people feel badly, often leaves them confused, and overall contributes to a culture of insecurity. If you've been ghosted enough times, it begins to feel like a person could just disappear on you at any time. People with abandonment trauma are particularly harmed by ghosting. Personally, I think the best way to handle wanting to stop talking to someone is to let them know in no uncertain terms that it doesn't feel like a good fit to you. You can wish them luck and get on your way. You can feel good about the whole exchange knowing you proactively and respectfully handled it.

Whoever sees the profile of a person they are interested in first should just write to them or "swipe right" or whatever! Don't wait for the other person to do it; it's flattering to show interest and initiative. Also, don't assume that if someone looks at your profile, or "likes" it, but doesn't reach out, that definitely means they aren't interested. Some people take a while to make a move.

Women seeking men, do not be afraid to message men first even when that is not the required protocol. Despite stereotypes, most men are not intimidated by women who make the first move; if they are, you may not be interested in them anyway! In my experience, I found that if I reached out first, the other person was pleasantly surprised that I'd taken that step. The logic is simple: everyone likes to feel desired. Despite pervasive stereotypes to the contrary, some masculine-presenting people are actually quite shy, as well. In fact, lots of people across the gender continuum are shy. So when you are courageous and reach out first, it spares them having to do that first step that might have been hard for them.

Furthermore, if you are a straight woman who wants an egalitarian hetero relationship, meaning one without too much adherence to traditional/stereotypical gender roles, why would you wait for the man to reach out first if you know you're interested? That seems silly to me. Just ask him out!

Once you start talking to someone, I would always suggest that you not message/text/email for too long before actually meeting in person. A few days or a week, tops. Because what happens if you do just message for a long time is that there is great potential to create a false sense of intimacy. You may start feeling like you really know this person and really like them... but then when you meet in person, if you don't vibe with them, it can create disappointment and confusion beyond what the situation warrants.

If you have to wait a long time for some reason before linking up in real life *(like there's a global pandemic, for example)*, make sure you talk on the phone a few times to try and mitigate that false intimacy. Do a couple of virtual happy hour meetings on your respective couches in order to foster some actual (close to real life) connection. And, of course, always be prepared for the real life person to not quite be what you'd imagined, whether for better or worse. In other words, don't get too attached to the idea of a person before you actually meet them. Be open to letting them show up differently than how you expect, and then decide how you feel.

On the first date, I would advise you to only go for a date that can be potentially cut short without much awkwardness. Meet for coffee or a drink. I would not suggest planning a whole day together, or even having dinner, because if you get there and you aren't feeling the person, you are absolutely not going to want to spend all that time. *(Trust me.)*

Also, on a first date, it's best to assume you're going to go dutch even if that's not how it plays out. Some people (often masculine-identifying people) are always going to insist on paying, and that's fine and appreciated. Personally, unless I sense there may be strings attached, I'm not going to argue too hard when my date insists on paying for my drinks. But femmes in this situation: you have to at least *offer* to pay for your own stuff, and be prepared to and totally fine with it if he agrees to split the check. Don't be that woman who expects the man to always pay. This isn't the dark ages and those norms are archaic. Not to mention, agreeing to the archaic norms that benefit you may indirectly signal that you're also agreeing to a lot of other norms that are far less beneficial to you.

Similarly, if he picks up the tab the first time you go out, I think that if you're financially able to, you should offer to pay next time, and mean it. It's a good reciprocal gesture. Reciprocity at every turn sets the stage for equity and relationship health. He may not let you, and that's your business, but I strongly suggest that you should at least offer, and be gracious either way.

That said, if you actually *are* that concerned about maintaining "traditional" gender roles, that too is your business. Just make sure you say that up front. Something like, *"I am a more 'traditional' kind of woman who expects men to be 'chivalrous' in certain ways,"* or *"As a man, I always pay because I think a woman should be treated a certain kind of way."* That's cool if you're into that; just make sure you don't present yourself as anything *else* or you're just setting both of you up for disappointment. As I said earlier, be wholly YOU from the first date and you'll be in a much better position moving forward.

As for same-gender or nonbinary couples, deeply-engrained stereotypes about gender roles can play out in all kinds of ways in any relationship. While navigating these dynamics maybe doesn't have these weird old rules *in the same way*, you will still have to work around some stereotypes. You will still have things to negotiate in terms of who pays for what, who takes on which role, and deciding what such things mean or don't mean for the relationship.

Next, and this should go without saying, there's definitely safety concerns when it comes to dating. First, make sure the first time you meet up that it is in a public place where you both *(but especially femme-bodied people, especially especially transwomen)* feel safe and comfortable. Next, do not give your address out on the first date. Do not have your date pick you up, no matter how "traditional" or "chivalrous" you all may be.

Do not go to someone's house for the first meeting. If your date does offer to come over or have you to their house on the first date, this is a potential red flag in terms of boundaries, worldly wisdom, and/or sense of self-pres- ervation. *(There are cases where this may be less relevant; I trust you to be wise and make good choices for yourself and read these as general guidelines.)*

I also advise everyone, but again, especially femme-bodied people *(because we all know it's a much more dangerous world for us),* that you always give a trusted friend your date's full name and the name of the location where you're meeting them. Send a photo if you can, even if that feels extra. You have to be mindful of safety because frankly this whole "meeting strangers" thing can be scary. Tell your friend that you'll text or call them when you get home safely. My best single friend does this with me, and then texts me the address if she goes back to his house. *(All this being said, if the whole purpose of getting together is for sex and you're both/all clear on that, then you may have to violate these general safety rules unless you can meet at a hotel or someplace neutral, which would be ideal.)*

Okay, so let's say the first date went great; you liked the person and would like to see them again. In this case, send them a quick text afterwards or the next day, directly stating as much. You don't have to go overboard. Just saying, *"I had a good time with you tonight"* or *"Can I see you again sometime soon?"* is sufficient.

This is a kindness that puts you on a healthy path because it eliminates space for game-playing, and removes that whole waiting period where you're just wondering, *"Do they like me? Should I follow up? Should I ask them out again?"* That waiting period can be stressful, and there's all kinds of arbitrary "rules" floating around out there about how long you're supposed to wait blah blah blah. In truth, the only "rule" should actually be what feels right to you, which I hope means telling them the truth, especially if it's that you liked them and want to see them again!

Conversely, if you did *not* like the person or would definitely *not* like to see them again, then just don't follow up. If they do, then a quick, *"Thank you, but I don't think we're a good fit. Best of luck!"* is a kind and completely acceptable response, vs. just ghosting them. In my opinion, it is rude not to respond to someone you have met in real life who is being kind to you. (Assuming the person is being kind.) But once you've said that, and been direct that you don't want to see them again, you don't owe them any further correspondence. *(And that is reason 2,945 why you never give a stranger your home address.)*

So those are my main dating tips. Most of them still apply even if you meet each other out in the world or are set up by mutual friends, so don't ignore this section because you're so opposed to dating apps. I warned you there would be cherry-picking required in order to get what you need!

# Reflection:

*List five adjectives to describe your feelings about dating.*

*When you read this advice, does it resonate with your lived experience about what dating is/can be like?*

*What do you like best about dating? What do you find scary, annoying, or frustrating about it?*

# LESSON 19: THERE'S SOMEONE FOR EVERYONE

The whole experience of strategizing and workshopping how to best and most authentically represent yourself on dating apps definitely gets me thinking that there has to be someone out there for everyone. Admittedly, there might be a very small subset of the population you are just right for, but I really believe there is someone out there who is looking for exactly what you have. (Always remember that there are *billions* of people in the world, so in some ways this is simply statistics.)

I was recently reminded of the adage, *"One man's trash is another man's treasure,"* which in this context means: what annoys, frustrates, or bores one person could very well thrill and excite someone else. So the person who thinks you're too sensitive, too emotional, or says you think too much, or whatever...screw 'em. There's someone else out there who will be amazed by your depth, your tender heart, and your active mind.

The person who thinks you're boring, or you never want to do anything exciting, or you're too comfortable with your little life...forget them, too. There's someone else out there who loves to Netflix and chill, who will happily go for walks and sit on the porch and read and be quiet with you. Or at least be cool with you doing things how you want to do them. It isn't necessarily required that a good-fit partner be how you are, just that they are accepting and supportive of it.

The thing is: you have to be honest about who you really are from the get-go, and clear on what you actually want in your relationships. Too often people present a cleaned-up, edited version of themselves in the beginning that isn't quite authentic. You may say what you think people want to hear, dress up more than you really want to, and maybe you agree to things you don't really want to do or wouldn't normally do. It's good to stretch yourself outside of comfort zones, certainly, but not to the extent that the stretch is not sustainable. If you're acting too far outside of your normal realm, you're going to get tired and eventually begin to drift back to your authentic preferences.

I understand the urge to do this "best foot forward" act, because who wants to just let it all hang out on the first date? You want to make a good impression. You want to make yourself appear "datable" or whatever. I totally get this. But the problem is, it's a lot of work to maintain a façade, and my whole point here is to get everybody feeling nice and easy*ish* in their relationships. Always remember: when you're in alignment and acting in congruence with your truest nature, things are more apt to feel easy.

Remember too that if you present a version that isn't quite accurate, when your truer colors bleed through, the person you're dating may rightly feel somewhat betrayed or misled. They may decide you can't be trusted, or that you're fake, or whatever. None of this may be true, but they don't know the real you, so they can't compare versions. They can't fact-check. They may just write you off instead, which would be a shame.

But if you show up as your full self from the beginning, they can be inspired to be their most authentic self as well. They can also make an educated decision pretty quickly as to whether they want to continue being involved with you. It saves you both a lot of time and energy in the long run.

But what if you're afraid to be your whole self? What if you don't really know who that is? Or, what if the real you needs some work? No problem. Go to therapy! I know I'm biased, and I know I keep saying this, but I promise it can really make a difference. Also, anyone worth getting involved with isn't going to judge you harshly because they find out you're working on your stuff. If they're healthy, they will understand the importance of getting help when needed. It's likely they have been to counseling at some point or currently see their therapist regularly as well.

Okay, so let's say you're still not happy with yourself, or you're still afraid to present your current iteration to a potential partner. Let's explore that. I suggest counseling first, but if mental health counseling isn't quite the ticket to get you where you want to be, try something else. Hire a life coach, spiritual advisor, career coach, or mentor. Identify patterns in your life that may be holding you back. Heal some old family relationships. You may need to change jobs so you can be happier. Maybe go back to school for a whole new career if that is what's in your way. Take medication if you need it. Take classes and learn a new language, or study something you want to know more about. Begin a new hobby. Start a meditation practice and expand your spirituality. Join a book club and start expanding your worldview through reading. Take CBD oil or get acupuncture or buy a weighted blanket so you can finally deal with the anxiety you feel. Try anything and everything. Be open to changing your life. *Own your shit.* And ultimately make the work of healing your wounds and getting actively happy your life's work because the world needs you!

Meanwhile, work on accepting and loving where you're at right now. Get comfortable with what parts of you are here to stay and what you don't need to constantly run from. You don't have to be perfect. *Perfection isn't even a thing, remember?* Scars are okay, you know; everybody who's had adventures has them. They make for good stories.

But, look, whatever you do: be the real you. All the time. Use all the lessons in Part One to help you determine exactly who that is, and then practice being that person with others. It will help you develop the kind of relationships that you want and deserve. Somebody is going to accept and love you for exactly who you are, in all your *(messy, strange, unique, beautiful)* glory. And you are then free to build exactly the kind of healthy, relatively easy relationship you both envision, whatever that may look like.

## Reflection:

*How do you tend to "show up" when dating?*

*Is it hard for you to be your authentic self?*

*If you're partnered, can any of this help you even in your already-established relationship?*

*Is there anything you wish you'd have known when you were dating?*

# LESSON 20: LET EVERYONE BE NEW

This is an important reminder when it comes to dating: the person you are dating or intimately involved with now is in no shape, form, or fashion to blame or be held responsible for anything anyone has ever done to you in the past.

I kind of want to repeat that for dramatic effect. I think I shall:

***The person you are dating or intimately involved with now is in no shape, form, or fashion to blame or be held responsible for anything anyone has ever done to you in the past.***

Everybody you date is brand new to you and deserves a clean slate. If you're holding onto grudges from past relationships, it is imperative that you do the work required to let them go. If you can't seem to let them go and move on, I would encourage you to get help to work on it, and perhaps be single for a while as you sort through things. It is fine to have stuff to work on, remember? It's just not fine to take it out on someone else.

Your new or current partner can't reasonably be expected to "pay" for whatever your previous partner has done to you. Okay? The relationship *will not work* if you start in a defensive stance, where you're just waiting and expecting that they will harm you. Despite possibly sharing a gender with previous partners, they are in all other ways an entirely separate and unrelated person. They have literally never done the thing(s) to you that your previous partner has done.

They may never do anything harmful to you in a million years, despite (maybe) your last partner being a complete asshole. Even if everyone you've ever dated was a complete asshole. *(That would merely suggest your person-picker is broken, not that everybody you could ever be attracted to is an asshole. So then we'd want to work on fixing the picker.)*

We often extrapolate based on our particular experiences. We might say, *"This is how women are"* or *"This is what men do"* or *"People suck"* (or whatever) and then treat our new person as though they are just an alternate version of the old person. But this is wildly unfair and always starts your relationship at a deficit. You will not be able to build a healthy, loving, respectful, honest relationship if you are holding on to grudges from previous partners and responding to your current partner as though they are to blame for any of that hurt.

The grace of a blank slate is something you should be offering all new people entering your life. Furthermore, doing the work to forgive anyone who has wronged you frees up space to allow the next person who comes along to be their own unique individual self. *(Leaving room for the idea that some people maybe do not deserve to be forgiven, like in the case of abuse and violence, for example.)* But generally speaking, I think this is crucial: you have to let every new person be new. If you're not ready for this, it's okay! Go back to the first section and do more work on you before you get into dating again so that you can do it well this time. Work through whatever you need to work through to be able to greet each new partner as the fresh potential they are. The easy*ish* relationship you want and deserve is waiting for you on the other side of the work.

# Reflection:

*Do you ever find yourself taking things out on your current partner that are residual from previous relationships?*

*How challenging or easy is it for you to let each person be new?*

*If it's easyish, how do you do it? If it's challenging, what gets in your way?*

*What steps can you take or have you taken to work on this?*

# PART THREE:

# MARRIAGE

# LESSON 1: WHY GET MARRIED?

S o you've been together for a while, and you may notice that people start asking you, *"When are you going to get married?"* (which, by the way, is a nosy and annoying question people should stop asking). For most people, it seems to be the next logical step for any serious relationship, but I think it is imperative to remember that you don't *have* to ever get married. I don't think marriage should be the be-all, end-all of relationships. You can live a perfectly happy life and never be married.

You might reasonably ask then, if I don't think marriage is a big deal or that important, why did I get married? I am happy to answer that for you, as it does provide context for my opinions.

First of all, my husband and I did things out of expected order, so there's no way to know what might have happened if we'd had a more traditional trajectory. We got pregnant and *then* got together. We had a kid and *then* got married. I don't recommend doing things this way! But in our case, it worked.

What is different and special about our relationship, and why I felt safe doing things in this somewhat reckless fashion, is that from the day I met him, I felt like: this person is my family. Actually, it's even more meaningful than that because I also feel no obligation to love him, because even though he's my daughter's dad, we could still co-parent and not be together. That factor doesn't obligate me to be with him romantically. *I actively choose him* as my partner every day. I am excited to come home just to be around him. I hate talking on the phone, but I often call him on my way to work to finish the conversation we were having when I left. Or just to chat. He sees me. He "gets" me. I see him, and I "get" him.

He is my person.

So because I felt so clear on the relationship, I didn't have the slightest qualms about tethering my life to his. That said, please notice I am intentionally using language like "tether" to describe the sensation associated with this marriage. I certainly don't think about it in the terms we often hear referring to marriage *(e.g., tied down, the ol' ball and chain, locked down, etc.)*

This is an important point because in a healthy, happy marriage, one should not feel at any point "tied down." The goal should be to feel "lifted up" and "set free" within the context of a loving relationship, whatever that context is for you and your person. (Remember, it just has to work for you!)

I mentioned previously that I've been married before, and that he was a lovely, kind man, and so it seemed like a good idea at the time. But what happened there was that very quickly I began to feel trapped, stuck, fenced in, and yes, *tied down*. It was nothing he was doing; I just learned too late that we weren't a good fit for a deep and abiding, free-feeling love.

To be honest, I'm grateful I had the self-awareness and gave myself the grace to end that as swiftly as I did, regardless of how painful it was at the time. I don't think going to marriage counseling would have helped. I don't think we needed to just "try harder, " and I don't feel like I owed the relationship anything I didn't give to it.

I remember that when I told him I wanted a divorce, he said, very calmly, *"Amy, you are the most self-aware person I know. If you've already decided, I know there is nothing I can do."* He didn't get angry or lash out at me; he was as kind in divorce as he was in marriage. We were just not a good fit, and we are both happier now. As hard as this may be to understand, from my perspective, it was a final act of care to leave him. It was also an act of self-love, because I knew this wasn't the place for me. I just wish I'd known it sooner, before we got married and had this big, expensive wedding. I never wanted to be divorced.

In my defense, when I got married before, I wasn't a marriage counselor yet, and I didn't have a lot of experience observing marriages from an intimate perspective. I had one very serious relationship prior to this, but obviously hadn't personally explored what it meant to be married. At the time, I thought I wanted to have a family and children, so I thought that meant I should get married. You have probably picked up by now that I'm not great at intellectualizing things without actually living them. And finally, I simply thought it was the thing I was supposed to do at the time I was supposed to do it, in terms of, you know, being an adult.

*Basically I didn't know what I was doing, and I made a big mess.*

I remember when I told my dad I wanted to get divorced. I was crying and upset and lamenting how I keep screwing things up. And he said, *"Babe, everybody makes mistakes. Yours just happen to be doozies!"* And we both laughed, because it was true, and/but I always learned from the mistakes and came out the other side stronger, smarter, and more clear on my path.

And so this is the first time I've been able to not only imagine, but to operationalize and *live in* marriage in the way I've always imagined it could be. What I have experienced in this relationship is the part I want to share with you. That is what I want for all of you: to only get married if it feels important to you, and then to have the best marriage *for you*, on your terms.

My husband and I are on a very realistic journey together. We discuss our relationship dynamics frequently. We rarely have conflict, but when we do, we work it out and reconnect before walking away from it. We are curious about each other and communicate well. (I'm sure it doesn't hurt that he's also a counselor, so we're both ahead of the game when it comes to communication and EQ.)

In short: *we are really good at doing this relationship.* So, couple that with having a child together, and suddenly marriage became a reasonable next step for us, if mostly for symbolic traditional reasons associated with "being a family." It is important to note that I sincerely enjoy being married to him, but that I also feel *entirely free* to be my most authentic self. Even if that authenticity at any point requires that we amend our agreements or even separate if it ever ceases to be good for us. I can't imagine that day, but I do trust that we would work together to make the decision that was best for us if it ever came to that.

So that's why *I* got married, but it's important to remember that people get married for all sorts of reasons, both practical and romantic. You may like the idea of choosing someone "forever," and want to symbolically announce your love to the world. You may not really care that much either way, but decide to get married for tax purposes. Maybe you feel like you found your "soulmate" and you can't imagine not making them your official spouse. Some people marry out of fear of losing, or desire to control, their partner. Maybe it's just that you've spent your life dreaming about marriage and family and so you jump at the first chance you get to make it a reality. Some people marry their first love, believing that first love to be the only true love. Some cultures practice arranged marriages, in which two families work together to create a situation that benefits the larger system.

All of these disparate situations (and many more I didn't mention) land in the same blanket category of "why people get married," but obviously there is no universal reason or answer. There are benefits to marriage, surely, but it's important to know that getting married (in and of itself) doesn't actually change the relationship at all. What I mean is: if things are feeling challenging on May 25 and you get married on May 26, you're going to wake up on May 27 and find that you're still in the same boat you were two days before, only it's now much more messy and expensive if you decide to break up. Just like how if it's awesome on May 25 and you get married on May 26, it'll still be awesome on May 27 and nothing will actually change.

I say this to say, think long and hard about why you're getting married, and what you're expecting it to be like. Discuss it with your partner so that your expectations are in alignment. Check in with yourself about how realistic those expectations are.

## Reflection:

*In your opinion, what are some valid reasons to get married?*

*If you're married now, why did you get married? How clear were you on your reasons at the time?*

*If you're not married, what are your thoughts about marriage? Do you want to be married someday?*

*What did/do you think will change or be different once you're married?*

# LESSON 2: MARRIAGE IS (JUST) A CONTRACT

One of my favorite things to remind couples in counseling is that marriage is really just a contract. Sometimes they look at me like I've insulted them in some personal way, and how dare I, but I am unbothered by their outrage. I think it's vitally important for people to understand and accept that that is *literally all a marriage is.* (Yes, even if you're religious; then it's a series of agreements you've made before your version of God and *also* witnesses.)

In agreeing to the terms of the contract on what is to forevermore be your "anniversary," the assumption seems to be that everything about it is permanent, as if a marriage covenant is some magically static and unalterable document. But the truth is, like any fair contract, the terms you have agreed to *can and should* be revisited regularly, and renegotiated as needed. In fact, I think a commitment to flexibility should be a requisite part of the original agreements.

When you begin to reframe a marriage as a contract, you are able to assess it more objectively and understand it as a living document that you can mold and change as often as is required to produce happiness. Think about it: the agreements you made when you were 25 are probably way different than the agreements you'd be willing to make if you were getting married at 40 instead. Right?

So then why in the world would you expect your 40 year old self to abide by agreements you made 15 years ago, before you were really even fully you? We could argue the nebulous question *"at what point we are fully formed,"* but I think *most* would agree that they are at least somewhat different in their wants, needs, desires, and values now than they were 15, 20, or 30 years ago. When I imagine myself at 25, I cringe to remember what seemed important to me then as opposed to what, who, and how I am at 40. I have done incredible amounts of growing and changing, and I feel certain that no agreements I had made then would feel relevant to me now, even if I'd stayed in relationship with that same person. To varying degrees, most people can be expected to grow and change over time.

So when entering into a marriage, beyond just taking the commitment seriously, I encourage you to be very intentional about what you are agreeing to. Do the agreements include the expectation of and right to change? Keep reading; I'll include some ideas for how to frame these agreements.

If you're currently married, but feeling unfulfilled or disconnected, consider broaching the subject with your partner of re-examining and possibly changing the terms of your marriage contract.

Here are some ideas for how to approach it:

*"Hey honey, I know we've both been feeling a lot of stress and strain in our relationship recently. Would you be willing to talk about things we can change that could make it feel better for both of us?"*

*"Babe, I don't want to get divorced. I think we can make this marriage work, but it's going to need to be a lot different than it has been. Are you open to hearing my ideas about what changes I'd like to see? I want to hear yours, too."*

*"Darling, this marriage has died and I think we need to build a new one. We haven't done a good job of navigating it together so far, but I'm not ready to give up. Can we find a counselor to help us?"*

You may roll your eyes at how simply I state this. You may truly believe it can't possibly be this easy and direct to start dealing with your relationship stuff, but…have you tried? *(Like, really tried.)* Have you tried setting aside your anger and resentment, or your need to be "right," or your desire to always have the upper hand, and just asked for your partner to join you in a real assessment of the relationship?

Some people would call this a "Come To Jesus" conversation, but that can seem threatening or scary. Ultimatums don't feel good to anyone, so I think framing it more positively is better. I would suggest that instead, you try thinking of it as "collaboratively dreaming up the relationship you both want." Or something like that. But whatever you call it, it's got to be offered in the spirit of reconciliation, grace, and a desire to forgive past transgressions. You both have to want to, consciously and with clear intention, move forward. If you can both access your highest self *(i.e., the very best version of yourself)* when entering into these conversations, you might find that there is a lot of healing just sitting there ready and waiting to happen. Someone just has to start the conversation.

My perspective is that it is never too late to make efforts you haven't made before. It is never too late to collaborate with your partner and amend the terms of the contract you've previously agreed to. Remember my basic tenets: there are no rules to relationships and they all have their own culture. As such, also remember that whatever agreements you and your partner make are okay and acceptable and even "healthy" if you have both conceded to them and are open and honest in the negotiations moving forward. My opinion is that many more marriages might survive if people were willing to get creative, collaborative, and vulnerable with each other about how best to continue, rather than just suffer for a while and then give up.

# Reflection:

*What do you think about the idea that marriages are really "just" contracts?*

*Does reframing marriage in this way give you any new ideas about how you could approach it differently?*

*Are there conversations about your marriage agreements that you should consider having with your partner?*

*If you're not married, how does this inform how you might approach marriage in the future?*

# LESSON 3: MAKE AGREEMENTS, NOT VOWS

Whard I think of the "vows" I might suggest you make to each other, they are miles from the traditional vows of "honor and obey" and stuff like that. Frankly, I find those very old-fashioned and sort of creepy. I'm not really judging if that's your thing, but I *am* requesting that you be a little bit curious and critical in your thinking about it. And I do want to strongly suggest that you expand your vision a bit. Marriage can be something different and greater than what the traditional notion of "vows" would suggest.

So let's think about that. *What if you were more focused on what you agree on from a practical, day-to-day angle rather than what you "vow?" How might that feel different or encourage different attitudes?* For example, here are some agreements my husband and I have made with each other. You are welcome to borrow them for use in your own marriage agreements if you'd like. Amend them to suit whatever specific vision you two have for your relationship.

I agree to be kind and compassionate to you.

I agree to hear you out and be willing to make adjustments when you have issues or complaints about our relationship.

I agree to always consider the impact of my behavior on you, and endeavor not to behave in ways that are likely to cause you harm or discomfort.

I agree to honor your stated boundaries, while understanding that boundaries can and do shift.

I agree to consult with you before making major decisions.

I agree to collaboratively parent our child(ren) with you, and to honor and respect you as a co-parent.

I agree to listen to you with an open mind at all times.

I agree to communicate with you in an intimate and vulnerable way to the best of my abilities, and provide space for you to do the same.

I agree to provide you with a safe place to be entirely yourself.

I agree to be my most authentic, honest, and true self with you.

I agree to inform you of any changes in my feelings toward you or about our situation.

I agree to be mindful of your needs, and do my best to meet them.

I agree to be open to revising the terms of our agreement at any time.

I think if more couples made agreements such as these, rather than old-fashioned traditional vows *(or perhaps in addition to, if they really want to do those too)*, and held themselves to the agreements, we might have more happily married couples. We would surely have more couples who are approaching their relationships as if they are the dynamic, ever-shifting, deeply human interactions they are.

Relationships are funny when you think about it. You just decide you really like a person and so you agree to spend a lot of time together and (probably) have sex with each other. Marriage is the ultimate act of "I really like you." It's like: *I like you so much I am agreeing to spend my whole life hanging out with you.*

I want to highlight that part -the "I really like you" part- and discourage the "ol' ball and chain" trope that gets people feeling stuck. No one is stuck, really, so I don't want you to focus on what you are giving up or losing by stepping into a marriage commitment. Instead, I want you to feel as if you are simultaneously completely free, deeply connected to your partner, and in enthusiastic agreement with them about the life you're building. I also want you both to know that you can and will grow and change within those agreements. I hope to arm you with the tools you need to navigate those changes. Ultimately I want you to feel confident that you can handle what comes your way and know that it will be okay.

## Reflection:

*How do you feel about the idea of agreements vs. vows? What are the differences, to you?*

*What agreements seem reasonable for a marriage?*

*How would you frame your marriage differently if you took this approach? Does this change your ideas about getting married in the future?*

# LESSON 4: YOU ARE NOT ACTUALLY (EVER) STUCK

**M**y friend and I were talking one day about relationships and why so many people languish in unhappy ones. She asked, *"What happens? Why are people so miserable? Why do they stay if they recognize it's not working?"* Off the top of my head, I had two main theories. See if you recognize yourself in either situation.

In the first, the relationship starts off great, and you seem like a good fit. You have some conflict but it doesn't usually turn into a big deal. You get married and everything seems fine.

Over time, small things happen (as they will) but one or both of you are not really equipped, able, or willing to deal with them in real time. So tiny conflicts may go unresolved, because it's just easier that way. Harsh words go unaccounted-for when spoken. Over time, you may or may not notice when you don't quite grow together during seasons of change. Things are still okay, but you don't really know how to communicate in a deep and vulnerable way.

Eventually, disconnection occurs one too many times. Erosion begins.

Fast forward 5, 10, 20 years…

You continue to stay because you can remember when things were better and you keep thinking and hoping you'll miraculously return to those days. The problem is you don't really know how to get there, because you didn't have the skills you needed to maintain it once things began to get harder. But there are enough good days that you cling to hope and you stay. *(By the way, hope doesn't heal relational wounds.)*

Eventually someone may stray, or someone may get fed up and leave. Maybe you try marriage counseling, which may or may not be helpful at this point. Either way, this is a sad outcome, because the two of you actually started off as a good pairing who "just" needed better skills. I say "just" in quotes because I will readily acknowledge that this can be daunting, and that for some people, learning these skills is not any easier than say, learning a foreign language or some complicated math. It requires diligence and effort, but it definitely can be done, and it can even feel satisfying and joyful.

*Insert strong suggestion here for seeking couples counseling in the early relationship stages, even if things aren't yet "bad." That's when radical preventive change can happen relatively easily vs. the challenge of years of clean up.*

The good news is that this relationship almost certainly *can* improve if you are both willing to learn new skills. You would have to commit to getting to know each other again, today, and re-connecting. It requires approaching the relationship with fresh eyes. Being able to accept that perhaps you have both been doing it wrong. Accepting that you have co-created this dynamic and that therefore, it's both of your responsibility to change it. Learning to communicate differently, to listen differently, to bypass your own and each other's defensiveness, and to radically forgive in real time.

It can happen! I've seen it. I've facilitated it. It's a thrill to be part of a rebirth like this, when a fundamentally sound relationship that is floundering at sea eventually rights itself. If you are willing to do the work, these *are* relationships worth saving. They are built on a solid foundation that's been eroding, maybe for years, but isn't yet crumbling. "Doing work" in this context is likely to have payoff, and to some extent be joyful and satisfying. In other words, even the work will be easy*ish*, and even if it doesn't heal everything, it will at least get you to a place where choosing to not be together is an active, respectful, and conscious decision, which is also okay.

Now, the second scenario is different. In this case, the relationship is laden with red flags from the get-go. It's challenging; communication is difficult and there are myriad dysfunctions and issues *(e.g., jealousy, anger, sexual issues)*. But you stick with it because you simply don't know that it should be easier than this or maybe because, romantically, you believe that love will magically heal everything. To quote that old Patty Smyth song, *"Sometimes love just ain't enough."*

Maybe you've never had or even seen a healthy relationship up close. Maybe you don't know that you deserve peace in your relationship. Or maybe you stay together because you are afraid to be alone. Or you stick with it because you got married and your values are such that once you make a bed, you lie in it…in perpetuity. No matter what.

Fast forward 5, 10, 20 years…(especially if you factor in children). By then, you have probably stayed and continue to stay because this dysfunction is familiar. You may not like it, but at least you know how to do it and what to expect from it. You don't even necessarily *dare to hope* things will get better, because "better" isn't a place you have been together. So you adapt to being unhappy. You live in perpetual conflict or, maybe worse, silence.

These couples are likely to be in what I call a "cold war." You mostly do your own things, you co-parent in parallel, your sex life all but disappears, you don't really talk much, and you may be one of those couples who make snarky comments about each other at gatherings *(which makes everyone else uncomfortable, by the way)*. When these couples come to counseling, it is always a last resort; it's the aforementioned "Hail Mary" or "Come To Jesus." There is usually evidence of all the Gottman® Four Horsemen: contempt, defensiveness, criticism, and stonewalling.

If this is your situation, I want you to know that I feel genuinely helpless when you come to my office because all I want to say to you is, *"Please do not keep doing this to yourselves and each other."* But I can't really say that, because you have the right to self-determination, so if this is what you want to keep doing, I always try to help. I try to help you unpack and unravel all the years of unspoken, unresolved hurt and conflict. But the problem here is that not only do you lack skills, but you may have been fundamentally mismatched from the beginning. If we're really being honest, you should probably never have gotten this far.

But in either case, it is crucial to remember that you are *not actually stuck*. There are conventions and there are legal considerations, but there is no actual mandate that you *must* stay together just because you got married. I know the intent of marriage is "forever," and nobody likes to think about divorce. But personally, as both a marriage counselor and a married person, I'm a huge fan of divorce. You know why? Not because divorce should be the quick and easy answer to a problem in your marriage, but because I believe in having choices. I appreciate having the right to determine the best path for my own life, and as such, divorce offers a choice. To be clear, I'm not advocating you get divorced, but I am always going to push people to fully consider all of their options before agreeing to live unhappily and in dis-ease.

So, I sincerely invite you to consider what the cost is of staying in a marriage that isn't serving either of you. If you're more like the couple in scenario one, there is potential for healing and growth and making it work. But if you're more accurately reflected in the description of couple number two, and you recognize the harm you are doing to yourselves, each other, and any children that you've brought into it, you have some hard talks and deep self-reflection to do for this lesson. Beginning with this basic concept: you are not stuck.

## Reflection:

*If you're in a relationship now, do you see yourselves more in couple one or two?*

*If you're couple one, what do you need to get your relationship to a place that feels better for both of you?*

*If you're couple two, what keeps you from moving on?*

*Do you feel stuck? What would it take to shift that feeling?*

# LESSON 5: TEACH YOUR CHILDREN WELL

L et's talk about what happens if you're married with children and things aren't going well. Let's say you're more like couple number two in the previous lesson. It seems clear that most often the issues began before you even got married, but were significantly amplified by the birth of children. So let's start there.

The most common scenario in a troubled "traditional" hetero marriage is this: beginning with the birth of the first child, the parents struggle to get on the same page and simply never recover. It can take many different forms, but there are some common themes. *(Note that I'm using "mom" and "dad" here and referring to the mom giving birth, but there is great diversity in the ways people bring children into relationships and each has its own unique set of stressors.)*

Sometimes it's that the mom feels -and is- totally unsupported in the experience of pregnancy and childbirth, because the dad simply doesn't "show up" for her. Full stop. This is a real phenomenon that women go through and I want to validate it if this was or is your experience. That sucks. It's scary and lonely to go through something so intensely transformative alone. Even worse somehow if you are technically partnered and "should" have support.

But oftentimes, it's a little more nuanced and we can offer a little grace in this case. Sometimes the dad just doesn't know what to do and freaks out. He's overwhelmed by some aspect of the experience. Given that so many men are under-skilled at communicating their emotional state, they may not know what to say about it and so they may fail to explain what is happening for them.

Sometimes it's that the mom is nursing, so the dad can't really help out at night; even though he can't really do anything at night, the mom nonetheless feels resentful that she is doing much more work and she's much more exhausted than the dad. Maybe the dad feels guilty that he's not really helping that much, but instead of saying so, he distances. Or sometimes the dad feels jealous that the mom and baby are bonding, and he feels left outside of that. He's used to getting attention and now suddenly all the attention is pointed at the baby and not him.

Or sometimes the mom is frustrated because the dad doesn't seem to realize how hard everything is on her. Sometimes it's that the dad just defaults to letting the mom lead the way, even though she is no more experienced at this than he is; actually, she wants the dynamics to feel more equitable. Or maybe she wants *him* to take the lead and not leave everything to her, and she either says it or doesn't, and it doesn't change. Maybe she is having some postpartum issues and needs additional care, but instead of showing up, he feels helpless and checks out.

Adding to this: everyone is completely exhausted (because new babies are kind of a nightmare in a lot of ways) and that makes them thin-skinned and unable to communicate effectively. Patience is in low supply. Most of the time, these dynamics continue without actually saying them out loud. Or else they are said but not with any real intention or skill at knowing what to do next. They weren't doing great at this before the baby, remember?

Of course, similar dynamics may unfold in same-gender relationships, too. It's just harder to delineate predictably like I can in hetero ones, since I've seen more of those up close. Also important to note that issues like these can and do arise in healthy relationships, as well. In general, I think most parents would agree that having kids is very hard on relationships under the best of circumstances.

Whatever the specifics, the common thread if you didn't (or don't) navigate this first birth well is that you never really find your way back to each other in any meaningful way. So the stage is set for the relationship to continue to struggle, only now you're significantly busier and more distracted, so reconnecting gets harder and can feel less and less important a thing to focus on.

So imagine you are coming to therapy after three kids and 15 years of this slow disintegration. Now, I am a very good marriage counselor, but I have a low success rate with couples under these circumstances. By that I mean it rarely gets much better. Believe it or not, you often do stay together, at least until "the kids are out of the house," but to me, that still feels like a failure. I don't know about other therapists, but my goal isn't always for the couple to stay together. I measure my success at helping them by whether they start making the changes they need, in order to move towards greater health and happiness, regardless of the ultimate outcome.

In fact, one of my first questions to couples is often: *Are you here to stay together, or to figure out whether you* should *stay together?* If they decide not to stay together, I can then help them navigate a "conscious uncoupling," as it were. Remember, I am a fan of divorce, insofar as it is important that you have options. Sometimes not being together anymore is clearly the best one.

The couples mentioned in the "You Are Not Actually Ever Stuck" lesson are two of the main archetypes I see in marriage counseling, especially long-married couples. And while the first *might* get better, the second almost certainly won't. So here is a radical idea: if you were to truly prioritize your own and each other's happiness, and you cannot figure out a way, despite your greatest and most sincere efforts, to make the relationship work, you would get a divorce already.

*Yes, even if you have children.*

I mean, yes, of course, if we're being honest you really shouldn't have stayed together in the first place once you recognized the challenges weren't abetting, but it is what it is at this point. It isn't ever too late to do better. I like to remind people that life is short and that you deserve to be happy. You deserve to be happy and to be in a relationship that meets your needs.

And so, when we talk about the kids, it is important to note that first of all, children are pretty resilient. Secondly, children tend to do better with happy parents. Third and most importantly, however, divorce does not have to be ugly or traumatic. It can be done well.

Now, please don't come at me as if I am underestimating the potential impact of divorce on children. I am not at all saying it will be easy or that it will have no effect on the children. I don't mean to suggest that this is a decision you should ever come to lightly. It is hard. But I *am* suggesting that the behavior we should all be modeling for our children is that we own our mistakes, we are adaptive to change when necessary, we take care of ourselves and other people, and we prioritize the happiness and health of the whole system. And if we are doing all of these things, the consequence may very well be that we determine the relationship we are in isn't working and should end.

There is a Carl Jung quote I especially like, *"The greatest tragedy of the family is the unlived lives of the parents."* This is powerful in its simplicity but also its controversiality. It's controversial because, in addition to the messaging we get about how we are supposed to work endlessly at relationships, we are likewise taught we should be completely satisfied by our roles as parents. This is particularly true for mothers, as if having children is going to "complete" us any more than finding the mythical perfect partner will. The truth is, it won't. It never does. It can distract, for years or even the rest of your life, and it can bring great joy, but it doesn't complete.

The fact remains you must be a whole person (or working towards this goal) prior to partnering or parenting, or you will always be over-relying on other people, including your children, to make you happy. Reminder: no one can *make* you happy. Moreover, it is not your children's job to fill your cup. It is an unfair burden to use them for this purpose, regardless of how pure your conscious intentions are. It is not their job to meet your needs for love or validation. Their only job is to be children.

Children require a lot of investment, much of which is unrewarded. Parenting can be overwhelming. Many parents simply do not want to martyr themselves for their families, but don't see another way because this sacrificial-style parenting, particularly for mothers, is so normalized in our culture. The resentment and the accompanying shame many parents end up feeling about the extent to which you are expected to sacrifice your own needs, desires, and dreams for your children and families contributes to many a dysfunctional household. It is hard not to be angry that you don't get to be a person once you have kids, but there's not much room to express these feelings in our culture if you have them.

The opposite but equally harmful scenario is when your entire existence becomes, willingly and joyfully, about your children and what they are doing. Once you have kids, you are not only not angry or resentful, you actually forget you even have your own feelings, needs, or wants.

But this is not a good plan, either, because not only is it not your children's responsibility to fill your cup, they have their own cups to learn how to fill. As they grow up, you have to leave plenty of space for them to explore who they are, independent of you. This is called "individuation" and it's a crucial aspect of adolescent development, even if you don't like it because it makes you feel lonely or disconnected from your child.

So you have to figure out how to continue to *be a person* throughout the process of raising children, and not just a parent, regardless of how you feel about it. If you're partnered, you must continue to be a partner as well. *(This is really about boundaries and enmeshment, so feel free to go back to that lesson.)*

You can relieve some of this parenting stress and tension, regardless of which style resonates more with you, by actively prioritizing your own, *individual adult human person,* happiness. Not at your family's expense, not like, *"I do what I want without regard for the impact on my family system,"* but as part of a fair and careful consideration of the wellness of the whole system. Because, as they say, *"When mama ain't happy, ain't nobody happy."* (Or daddy). You cannot cease to exist because you are a parent, even if you do so willingly and joyfully.

This may be radical, but I think it's crucial that you model for your children how to advocate for yourself, how to respectfully ask for your needs to be met, and how to establish and maintain boundaries. Kids need to see that you love and respect yourself (and your partner) enough to walk away from a situation that is harmful to you. They need to see you rebuild a healthier situation, even if they can't really understand what they're seeing at the time.

You do not model these good things when you "stay together for the kids," especially when you're also showing them, subtly and not-so-subtly, how unhappy you are to be making this sacrifice. I personally think you do your kids a profound disservice when you force a marriage to sustain for *x number of years* or *until the kids are out of high school,* and then abruptly announce that you are divorcing. That's actually more disruptive in some cases, as your kids may start to wonder if their whole life was a lie. (I know it sounds dramatic, but this is a real risk.)

*Of course* you're worried about the impact a divorce will have on children, and as I said before, it is wise to fully consider your options. There is no good time to do hard things. There's always another birthday or holiday coming up, or some landmark of childhood, that makes it seem a bad time to do something intensely disruptive. The last thing you want to do is harm your kids. Every decision we make once we have kids is infinitely weightier than the ones we made prior. But the truth is, if there is never a good time to do hard things *(and what is harder than breaking up a family?)* then at some point you have to just rip off the bandaid and do the thing. Stop gathering evidence and just make the move.

So yes, divorcing will almost certainly have *an impact of some kind* on the whole family system at any stage, but if you know you're making yourselves and the whole family miserable by staying together, I would invite you to consider that perhaps you are not doing your kids any favors. The impact of staying together may be far more damaging than the impact of divorce. Your kids may be in therapy 20 years from now, not, as you might predict, lamenting their parents' divorce, but lamenting instead that they've never seen a healthy relationship. I have counseled these people. They are not okay. They struggle with relationships as adults, they have trust issues, and they often name their parents' dysfunctional relationship dynamics as part of their root issues. Often, when I ask if their parents are still together, they say, *"They are, but I don't know why. They're miserable."* The quality of the relationship is what the kids feel, notice, and remember in their bones. Not just whether you stayed together.

## Reflection:

*Do you think people should stay together for the kids? Why or why not?*

*What lessons do you think you're teaching in either case (staying together or divorcing?) Which lessons do you think are more useful for children?*

*If you are in a situation like this, what are your reasons for staying or going?*

# LESSON 6: DIVORCING WELL

As I've mentioned, I am not typically in the business of peddling "should"s, as everyone is different and everyone has the right to self-determination. This is a social work term that means *"at all times you have the right to decide what is best for yourself."* But this is one "should" that I believe is really important: I am writing this book because I want people to know that relationships should be, and that they can be, fundamentally easy. Easy*ish*. You should not have to constantly work at them.

I know our culture loves to promote the idea "marriage is hard work;" that idea has been baked into how we do relationships such that we rarely question its accuracy. But I think it's harmful to expect marriage to be such hard work. The way we've normalized putting Herculean effort into sustaining your marriage encourages people to stay when they should go, because we love to praise hard workers. But what is the point of working hard just to constantly fall short? (Serious question.)

Let me say it this way: Not every relationship has potential for long-lasting happiness, no matter how much love and effort you pour into it. Some combinations of personalities are just not going to ever be restful and safe and easy-feeling. *Sometimes you are just not a good fit.* There is no shame in admitting you tried and it didn't work. The first two parts of this book are designed to help you get to marriage in a healthy way, so that hopefully once you get there, you can stay and find (relative) ease and happiness. But if you're there already and it's not going well, I am intent on helping you either do what you need to do to heal, or find the strength and wisdom you need to walk away. I am not here to shame people into staying married, as though marriage is the ultimate achievement regardless of how happy you are.

Anyway, obviously, of the two situations mentioned in the preceding lessons, scenario one (where it was once good and could be good again) is preferable. But I hope what you're starting to see as another possibility is one where you begin in a healthy relationship, and as you see things come up, you address them in real time. In this best case, you also get help when you don't know how to handle something or when you find that you continuously fall short. You don't have to go through years of suffering first. If you're attuned to these factors, you also recognize when it's time to move on, if that time comes. You know when to fold 'em, as it were.

There is nothing sadder to me in my work than seeing couples harm each other out of fear and hurt and built-up resentment. Or seeing couples who just aren't a good fit struggle against their basic natures just to stay together "no matter what." As I've said before, people can change behaviors, but they can't change who they are at their most fundamental.

My thought is: if who you are is not compatible with who they are, do you really want to spend your whole life in struggle? Refer back to the lessons on compatibility, and about what makes you YOU, and about whether the things that you love about yourself are the same things your partner loves about you.

If you're married and either of these two scenarios is resonating with you, think a little more about whether you feel stuck in the current relationship, and why this might be. *What makes you feel like you can't or shouldn't leave? Are the sources of this reluctance internal or external?* Name the fears that keep you feeling as though you do not have options, or that your option to leave isn't viable. There are some very real issues that arise when people consider leaving long-term relationships, especially marriages where there are shared assets, debts, children, enmeshed extended family dynamics, or religious pressure.

Sometimes a person is simply not financially positioned to leave, despite a strong desire. This is particularly tragic, and I'd invite you to consider all of your options, even undesirable ones like borrowing money or living with a parent while you get on your feet. And yes, of course I know it is a privilege to have any of these options, and sometimes there is simply no choice. In which case, work on figuring out how to find as much happiness, safety, and peace as possible in the current situation. Harm reduction is viable as a last resort.

But in the absence of severely limiting circumstances, mostly just think about whether you are actively choosing to be there everyday, with this specific person. *Are you there because you intentionally and fully want to be there?* Ask yourself whether this is the life you want to be living, especially if you believe it is the only one you get.

If the answer is that the relationship simply does not feel right for some reason or another, but decidedly so: please consider the idea that you are actually not stuck, obligated, or beholden. The healthiest relationships are the ones where we feel free to leave at any time, but we consistently, every day, choose to stay because it is the very best place we can imagine being.

What I tell clients when they come in: I am here to help you heal your marriage, if that is your intention. That said, if you are unable to renegotiate how you are agreeing to love each other, I would fully support helping you separate respectfully and with kindness. Many therapists will effectively "shame" people into staying married, particularly if children are involved, but my approach is more pragmatic.

I say: Let's look at what's going on and be realistic in our assessment. If you can return to a place of happiness in your marriage, by all means, do so. I can offer you skills for conflict resolution and tips on how to communicate better. You can practice and work on things. You can have more sex. You can spend more quality time together. You most certainly owe it to yourselves to do everything you can to ensure you've dotted your i's and crossed your t's, especially if you have kids. Your kids deserve your best effort.

But if you do everything you know how to do, and you still find yourselves unable to reconnect…if it remains just too hard to trust each other, to be vulnerable, to put your love into action, and to consistently live in alignment with your highest selves, then my thought is: do one another one last kindness and put your marriage down. A metaphor I often use is that divorce done well is done much the same way you'd euthanize a beloved family pet who has been long-suffering. It may be macabre, but that's really what it is: a death. But when done with ritual, sadness, grief, and understanding that it is for the best, it also holds a little bit of beauty. I think it is important to contextualize "divorce done well" as a final and very difficult act of love, not as a failure.

I don't at all mean to trivialize the pain of divorce (or any relationship ending after some length of time and commitment). I hope that is clear. I believe in marriage, as evidenced by my own agreements and commitments. I will do everything I possibly can to ensure that my daughter grows up with two happy parents, and I'd prefer that we all live together throughout her childhood. But I also believe in freedom and choices, and am comforted by knowing I don't *have* to stay if it becomes untenable. That freedom makes my choice to stay every day feel like intention.

But what I often see in counseling is people feeling stuck. Believing you do not have any options but to learn to live with suffering. I believe that divorce offers a choice that many people do not feel permitted to access. I'd like to offer you permission to consider that maybe the ultimate act of love is to set each other free, and that there is no shame in any of that.

## Reflection:

*What do you think about the idea of "divorce done well?"*

*What are your opinions about divorce, in general?*

*How much reframing would it take for you to think about divorce as an act of kindness vs. "giving up?"*

# LESSON 7: CONCLUSION & NOTES FOR CONTINUING EDUCATION

I hope you found this book useful. I hope that at the very least, it gave you some new ideas and ways to think about relationships. I know I've asked you to stretch, and that can be uncomfortable or even painful. If you've stuck with me, I know you're up for the challenge. That's what this is all about, after all: learning, growing, and changing. You may never "graduate" from all of this, and that's okay, because there's always more to learn about yourself and the people you love. I am still learning, myself. This book may be revised many times in the future as I learn more.

I began with the premise that none of us really know what we are doing, and that we can all benefit from learning new skills. I wanted to offer you what I have learned the hard way, so that maybe you won't have to go through quite as much. It took me a very long and twisty road to get to easy*ish*. I hope your path is smoother than mine was.

This book is a place to practice knowing and loving yourself, in order to be able to translate that knowledge into knowing and loving another person (or people, for my poly readers). If you then choose to elevate the relationship into a healthy and happy marriage, cool. If you don't, that's fine too.

Also, if you decide after reading this that monogamy is not for you and you want to always have multiple partners, that's your business and I support it fully. If you read this and decide that, actually, now that you mention it, *dating is for the birds and you don't want to ever do it,* okay! You can still benefit from the work in part one. If now you are going to go travel the world solo and not be burdened with intimate partnerships, whether for a while or indefinitely, good for you. If you've been afraid to step back into the world of dating, I hope this gives you some hope that there's someone out there who's right for you. If you've been together a long time and realize that marriage sounds like a healthy next step you're prepared to take, I'm excited for you. If you're long-married and after reading this realize that you've been longing to get a divorce for years, I hope this gives you the strength to advocate for yourself and move on.

Whoever you are, whatever you do, always remember that the journey is the work, and that happiness is not a place. Marriage is not a beginning or an end; it's merely part of some people's relationship story. It's not for everyone, and even if you do go there, you can always come back. Your life and your path are yours. If it's working and you're happy, it's "normal." You can build it how you want it to look.

My goal in life is to help more people in the world be intentional and wise about the efforts they put into relationships, and increasing the overall happiness quotient. We could all use more happiness, radical grace, and relative ease. Thank you for taking this journey with me!

Happy Learning!
~Amy~

PS If you enjoyed this book, I'd be eternally grateful if you posted an honest review wherever you buy books.

PPS Email me directly at amy@millercounseling.org and/or follow me on FB @Millercounseling.org or IG @MillercounselingIG. I also write a blog occasionally at patreon.com/amymiller. If you're interested in working with me for Relationship Coaching based on the principles in this book, my website is millercounseling.org and has more info.

# APPENDIX: TIPS & TOOLS FOR DOING CONFLICT WELL:

1. Only fight about what you're actually fighting about. It's wildly unfair to bring up old stuff. Have a separate conversation about whatever residual thing you might be reacting to, but be clear that *this* is about a specific thing and that is the thing to focus on. If your fight is really about several things that have been layered on top of one another, take the time to consciously separate them out. If you're actually upset because of something else entirely, be mindful enough to say, (once you realize it): *"You know what? I'm over-reacting right now because I've been feeling neglected lately (or whatever the thing is). This isn't really about _____, but more about _____. Can we talk about that?"*

2. If something comes up that is clearly unrelated, but troublesome, you can realize it out loud, literally stop the conversation, and make a note to talk about the other thing later. Sometimes there are many layers to our frustration, sadness, anger, etc. Think of long-term resentments as onions; when you peel away a layer that's about *this*, you find underneath there's a layer that's about *that*. It can take a while to sort it all out and figure out how you really feel and what's important to hash out.

3. Being able to recognize that you're actually upset about a lot of things/ other things and being willing to set them aside to resolve *this thing here right now* demonstrates that you're intentionally positioning disagree-

ments and conflict as conscious and productive, rather than just...
needing to be mad. This shows that this thing you're actually upset
about today is uniquely important and deserves attention, rather than
it's just the overflow of general irritation you haven't addressed yet.

4.   Always use "I" statements. This is a basic one, but it may help to
remind us all to use "I feel _____ when you_____" *instead of* "You made
me feel _____ when you _____". This will naturally make the argument
feel less like an attack that requires reflexive defensiveness.

5.   Even better than that is *"When _____ happens, I feel _____ "*. It's a minor
shift, but this phrasing puts a little padding between the action and
your feelings and the other person, which can be helpful. It specifically
does not blame the other person for your feelings about what they did.
Even if the other person is clearly responsible for the action, this allows
the action *(the thing that happened)* to be a separate topic, which can also
help defuse potential defensiveness.

6.   To the best of you abilities, be 100% honest and direct about how
you feel and what you want. It doesn't pay to beat around the bush.
Say what you need to say as clearly as possible. It may not come out
perfectly, but that's okay. Make sure it at least gets out. You can sort
it out later. But don't say one thing that is only partially true only to
have to correct yourself or elaborate later when you get the courage,
because that can cause the other person to doubt your veracity overall.
You have to be someone to be trusted in this way.

7.   Practice reflective listening. If you're not sure you get exactly what the
other person is saying, reflect it back to them for clarification, like this:
*"This is what I think you're saying, is this right?"*

8.   If something landed poorly on you, it's entirely possible you misunderstood or they misspoke. In the heat of the moment, it's hard sometimes
to sort out what you want to say and how you really feel. Sometimes

we say it wrong. So don't fly off the handle immediately. Make sure you give them a chance to correct you before you react.

9.  Immediately (like right now) stop using global words like "Always" and "Never". Nobody really "always" does something and nobody really "never" does something. Rephrase it. Say, *"Sometimes you x and it bothers me"* or *"I've noticed that it's rare for you to y"* or something like that. Anytime you use "always" or "never," the other person is immediately going to get defensive and go digging for a time that whatever the thing was was not the case, which they will usually be able to find, because... nobody "always" or "never" does anything.

10. Make sure you're not shutting the other person down, especially if they are quieter or less comfortable with conflict than you are. Don't talk "at" anyone. Stop, and ask them to respond if/when you realize you've been rambling or have accidentally shut them down. Wait for it if they need a moment to collect their thoughts. Be patient and allow the other person to carefully deliver their thoughts and feelings in whatever way works for them.

11. Talk about the behavior, not the person. Say, *"I don't like when you do this"* not, *"You're such a _____"*. Any time you present your complaint as though it's an indictment of the person rather than the action, you're going to get a defensive reaction. (**REMEMBER**: the main objective of fair fighting is to eliminate the defensiveness that tends to accompany conflict.)

12. Obviously it should go without saying that you cannot name call. At all. Ever. If any relationship you're in contains name-calling, immediately make a mutual vow to stop it. Period. People can get into some pretty ugly habits, but remember that these are just behaviors and can be interrupted with mindfulness. But this is a non-negotiable one because basic emotional safety includes no risk of being called names. Keep in mind too that *emotional violence is still violence.*

13. Do not curse (at people as in name-calling, but also just in general) when you're fighting. It's an automatic elevation of whatever the discussion is. I love curse words as much as the next guy, but I make a conscious effort to avoid them when I'm engaged in any kind of conflict or difficult discussion. There's a big difference between *"You hurt my feelings"* and *"You fucking hurt my feelings, you fucking asshole."* See?

14. One might think this should go without saying, but do not drink alcohol while you're attempting to resolve some major issue. It doesn't help. You may think that it lubes you up to be able to say stuff more easily, but you're way better off stumbling through it sober than trying to piece together what the conversation was even about the next day. You'll miss nuances if you're drinking, for sure.

15. Make sure neither of you are standing over the other (or doing anything else with your body that might make the other person feel smaller than you or disempowered) when the conversation happens. Sit down facing each other in a quiet place. Whenever possible, make conflict intentional. I realize you sometimes (often?) just get in a fight spontaneously, but generally speaking, we know when there is trouble brewing with someone we are close with. Handle it. Sit down.

16. Sometimes people are just loud talkers anyway, but most of us tend to get louder when we are upset. Make a conscious effort to lower your voice. Yelling at each other doesn't actually help either of you hear each other better. In fact, it tends to have the opposite effect. Next thing you know you're just shouting and not listening at all.

17. If you're fighting with a partner or loved one, it can be very therapeutic, if somewhat challenging, to pause a fight and physically connect in some way. Either hug, or hold hands for a moment, or kiss, or something that reminds you that you actually really care about each other. It can be a powerful grounding experience. Again, it is also really hard because sometimes when we are in our feelings, we would much rather

punch them in the face than hug them. Hence, this is something to practice and strive for. It does work, though, if you can get there.

18. I realize this won't always be possible, but when you can, limit your discussion/disagreement/fight to no more than 30 minutes. There is no reason to stay up all night hashing over the same thing. It's not going to be helpful once you get to a certain point, and especially if you're tired. If you can't come to a resolution in 30 minutes, agree to do whatever you need to do to be able to take a rest from it until the next day and revisit it then. Don't just beat a dead horse all night, go to bed angry, and then have a shitty text fight all day the next day. (Remember: Do not have any important conversations via text!)

19. This is a very basic thing that a lot of couples do anyway, but it's legit: **DO NOT GO TO BED ANGRY.** That doesn't mean you totally solve all your problems every night before 11 p.m., but make sure you reconnect in some way before you go to sleep. Even if it's to say, *"Look, I'm still mad at you, but I love you and I know we will work this out. Goodnight."*

20. If your partner reaches out to you to repair whatever happened, whether during or after the conflict, you cannot ignore it. Sincere repair attempts must be acknowledged and honored. It doesn't mean that your partner can just be like *"Sorry"* and you have to pretend nothing happened, but it is important to at least acknowledge the attempt.

21. Don't repeat yourself. If you have already said something, clearly and succinctly, and you have reason to believe the other person heard and understood it, there is no reason on earth to say it nine more times. Repetition of the same point is not how to reach resolution. It is most likely going to simply annoy the other person.

22. However, if they are truly not understanding the point you're trying to make, and you believe it is important to the overall conversation, try to say it a different way and see if that works. We all have different communication styles, and sometimes the way we say things doesn't

convey to the other person what we are really trying to express and so we need to try explaining it another way. Sometimes a few different ways.

23.  Likewise, be sure to respond appropriately to what the other person actually said/is saying. Don't have parallel conversations where you're actually not even talking about the same thing. If you find yourselves doing this, stop the conversation and acknowledge that it's happening. Say, *"I'm realizing we aren't really talking about the same thing. Can we clarify what we are actually trying to discuss?"*

24.  Work together, not against each other. You cannot strive for winning an argument. That's not how it works in real life, in respectful relationships. The goal is always a win/win. Find a solution everybody is okay with. Neither of you may get exactly what you were after, but compromise is how you resolve and move forward. Remember that if you are in any kind of ongoing relationship with one another, you are on the same team. It would behoove you to act like it.

25.  If one or both of you starts to lose your temper and escalate to some unforgivable next-level stuff, take a break. Call a time-out. Allow each person this opportunity at any point, and honor the request. You don't get to be like, "No, we are not taking a time out because you have to listen to me right now." That's not how we do conflict well. That is not how we honor people we care about. *(Remember the idea "I love you too much to have this conversation right now.")*

26.  Understand that in the height of real-time argument, people are going to say things they don't mean or say things differently than they might if they had more time to craft a response. Obviously, the goal is to avoid this, but as we are learning how to do conflict better, it's still likely to happen. Grant the other person the grace to retract something they didn't mean or to rephrase something they may have clumsily stated. Don't get so literal that you hold them accountable

for every syllable they utter and punish every misstep. (You don't want them to do this to you!)

27. Manage your facial expression. Do not roll your eyes or make faces at the other person. If you've been told your face is extremely transparent, and you find yourself communicating with your face or eyes while the other person is talking, stop it. Rein your face in. Specifically, nobody appreciates eye-rolling. It's a very clear way of communicating contempt for what the person has said, and there's no place for it in healthy dialogue of any kind.

28. Passive-aggressive behavior must be avoided altogether. If you have a thing to say, say it. Do not make the person guess what you mean, or pretend to be joking when you are clearly not joking just because you feel vulnerable saying whatever you feel. Don't say "It doesn't matter" or "Whatever" or "It's fine" when those are clearly not the things you're attempting to express. (Revisit the lesson about passive-aggressive behavior if you need to!)

29. If you feel like the other person is being passive-aggressive, provide a space where you can gently discourage it. You can say, *"No, not nevermind! Let's talk about this. It's clearly something that's on your mind."* or *"What are you trying to say? It's okay to say whatever it is. I want to understand where you're coming from and how you feel."*

30. Do not include other people's opinions in your complaints (e.g., *"My friends all think ...."* or *"I know your mother agrees with me,"* etc.). This is a passive-aggressive way of making the other person feel unduly judged, or of activating shame, or of not just owning your own opinion. Whatever your actual (conscious or unconscious) intention, just don't do this. Your own opinion is sufficient to have a discussion around.

31. Use appreciative, affirming language whenever possible. Even when you are frustrated or angry, there is still a need to be respectful and loving to the other person. If you make a point that is important to you,

and it is not met with argument, or your partner says, *"Okay, that makes sense to me,"* that is cause enough to acknowledge: *"Thank you for hearing me and conceding my point. I appreciate that."* This may sound inauthentic until you fully integrate it into how you do conflict, and then it just becomes part of your repertoire.

32.   Sometimes, just stop. Give up. Recognize this is not a thing to be solved today. If the argument is fruitless and circular, there are times you have to just call it a wash and walk away, at least for a while. And if you just stop fighting, the other person will too. It's impossible to fight with somebody who isn't fighting back.

33.   Remember: conflict is not inherently bad. It doesn't have to be scary. It doesn't have to be threatening to the relationship. It is merely a way of coming to resolution. It can be extremely useful and enlightening. The better you get at doing it respectfully and kindly, the less scary it will seem.

34.   Keep in mind that you can only take responsibility for your half. A common question is, *"Well, what if I learn how to do it well but the other person refuses to? What's the point?"* The point is *you* are doing it well. You can't control the other person's response, but what you can do is set a consistent example for how to disagree respectfully and with kindness. You can be a person others are not afraid to be honest and engage deeply with because they trust that you will respond appropriately.

# ACKNOWLEDGMENTS:

Asya Blue of Asya Blue Design (asyablue.com) designed the book and took it beyond my wildest dreams.

Alison Green designed my websites and has my eternal gratitude for making me look good online.

Michelle Evans is responsible for my beautiful author photo (and our family photos this year!) michelleevansphotography.pixieset.com

Dr. Amber Johnson, professor, activist, artist, and founder of The Justice Fleet, is where I first heard the phrase "Radical Forgiveness." They have also been super supportive of this project. Thank you and I love you!

Becky Vollmer created an online community called "You Are Not Stuck" that is congruent with my perspectives and inspired the lesson here by that name. She's from St Louis and she's rad; check her out. youarenotstuck.com

Thank you to my excellent beta readers who were brave enough to give me critical feedback; it changed how this book turned out and made it better.

All quotes included here are either in the public domain or have been permitted by the author or the publisher.

# REFERENCES & THINGS TO GOOGLE:

Author and shame researcher, Dr. Brené Brown (brenebrown.com) is the leading voice on vulnerability, shame, and courage.

Marge Piercy's poem "The Implications Of One Plus One" as well as my other favorite, "To Have Without Holding," will blow your mind.

"Tiny Beautiful Things" by Cheryl Strayed is an amazing and inspirational book. She personally responded to my request for permission to quote her.

John & Julie Gottman of The Gottman Institute (gottman.com) are leading marriage researchers; you may appreciate finding a couples' counselor who use The Gottman Method. I completed the first level of their training and found it useful.

Myers-Briggs Type Inventory® (MBTI®) is a system of personality typing based on the theories of Carl Jung. I'm certified in MBTI® and find it fascinating. (myersbriggs.org)

Gary Chapman wrote a whole series on The 5 Love Languages® (5lovelanguages.com)

Made in the USA
Monee, IL
28 September 2022

14832290R00152